AN ANGEL LIVED IN OUR HOME

2018

RAFA: AN ANGEL LIVED IN OUR HOME

by Nivaldo Nassiff, PhD

Published by Rafa Legacy.
For more information, contact our corporate/institutional sales department (617) 908-5966 or

rafalegacy2018@gmail.com

Editor:

Alberto Matos

Translated by:

Josias Souza

First Revised by:

Julie Souza

Second Revised by:

Eluzai Chaves

Cover:

Elton Pretel

Graphic Concept and Design:

contact@pelicelistudio.com - Toronto, ON - Canada

Printing History: 1ª. Edition – November 2018

Manufactured in the United States of America.

ISBN-13:978-1986485999

ISBN-10:1986485994

AN ANGEL LIVED IN OUR HOME

Nivaldo Nassiff, PhD

ORLANDO, FL
2018

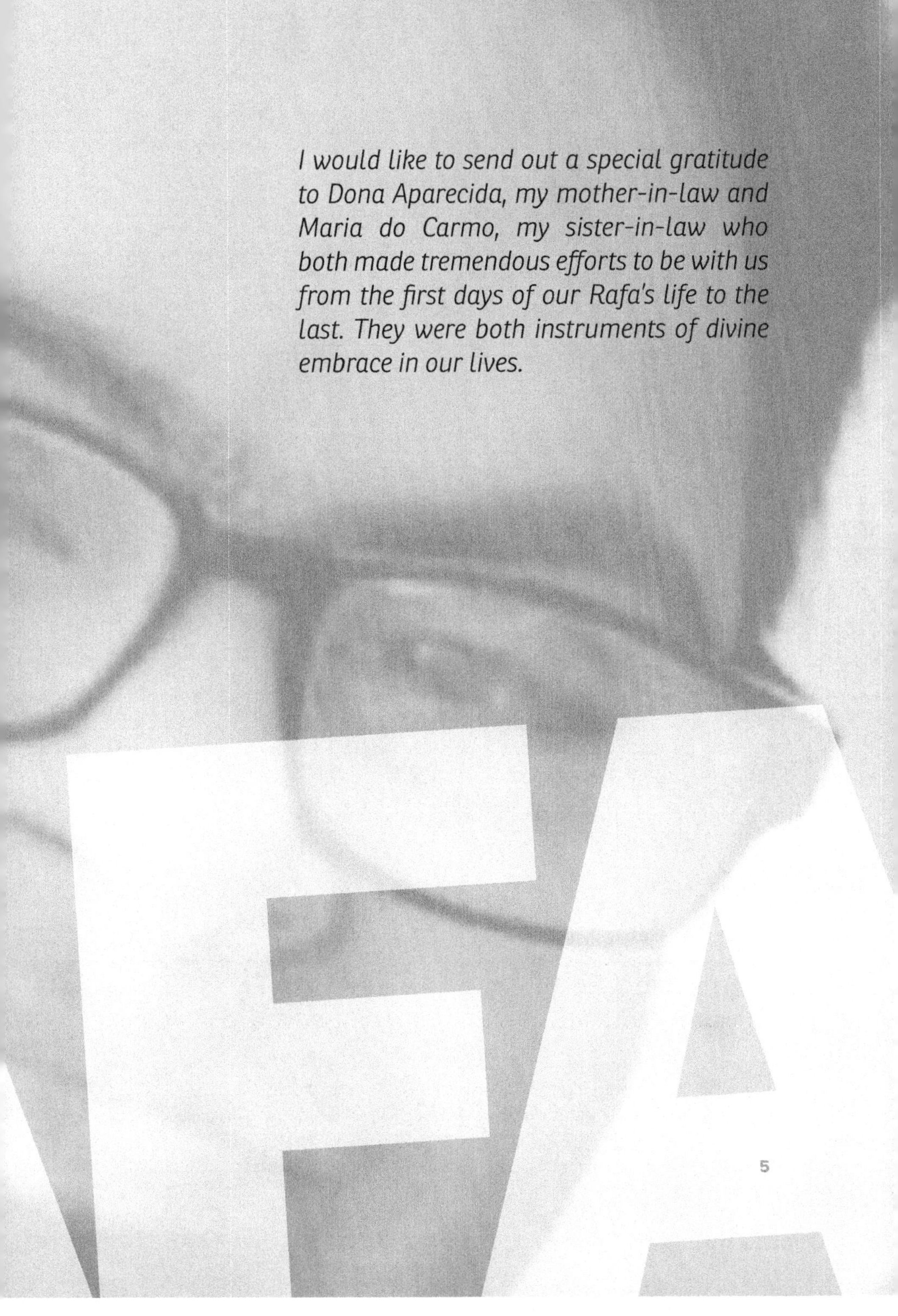

I would like to send out a special gratitude to Dona Aparecida, my mother-in-law and Maria do Carmo, my sister-in-law who both made tremendous efforts to be with us from the first days of our Rafa's life to the last. They were both instruments of divine embrace in our lives.

I would like to share my gratefulness to Sofia Pupo the"adopted one".

Rafael chose to adopt our great friend Sofia as a member of our family. In everything we did as a family, Rafa always reminded us to include her. Sofia loved Rafa with an overpowering, extravagant and constant love. Thank you Sofia for being the "adopted one" of our family.

FA

Epigraph

Do not forget to show hospitality to strangers, for by so doing some people have shown hospitality to angels without knowing it **– Hebrews 13:2.**

By faith Abel brought God a better offering than Cain did. By faith he was commended as righteous, when God spoke well of his offerings. And by faith Abel still speaks, even though he is dead **– Hebrews 11:4.**

Contents

Endorsement

Nivaldo pulls back the curtains of pain and exposes us to the raw reality of losing his son. As he parallels his heartache with stories from the Bible we see the true nature of how we must all deal with pain and suffering in our life. As his pastor for six years, I've had a front-row seat to the incredible story of Rafael. But even more, I've watched his parents walk through this with a broken heart and with a faith that has held them together. Their story is one we all need to hear and their hope is one we all need to have. In this book, Nivaldo shares "My pain is temporary, because my Savior, because of His grace (only that and nothing else, nothing in me, because there is nothing good or acceptable in me), guarantees me the eternal reunion with my son. And so, I will never again be torn apart." God bless you Nivaldo and Lucia, thank you for telling your story.

David Uth, Ph.D.
Senior Pastor
First Baptist Orlando

Prologue

"Love must be sincere."
Romans 12:9.

After reading and re-reading this book several times, I feel privileged to recommend it. I saw myself inserted, like a character, in each narrative, observing everything and learning. How have I learned!

These pages are an invitation to meet an extraordinary worshipper and servant of the living God, one who saw no impossibilities, who has impacted people in the past as much as he will in the present and future.

It is a story about deep reciprocal love, without hypocrisy, reflecting the complicity in relationship of parents and children who love each other with no limits. We are challenged to a deep reflection on how to measure the commitment and surrender of parents for the sake of their children. How to sacrifice selfishness and exercise altruism, in its sweetest and deepest essence. How to deal with the discrepancy between what is ideal and what can be accomplished. It is an extraordinary and fun narrative about the complicity of love in the production of a beautiful and permanent fruit. We will reflect on life and its surprises, relationships at home, at church, and above all, with the eternal Father.

We will see the Nassiff family progressing in dealing with finding the best course of action to educate and care for their "angel," and how they were surprised day by day with the teachings of someone so special.

Many preconceptions, and even "indisputable" concepts, are put to the test. And what a test it was! Human weaknesses are exposed without any constraint before the Almighty God. The one who sees and knows everything and who can do anything.

We will see that the constraints, often imposed by the unwholesome society in which we live, unravel at the privilege of having and recognizing God in our home.

The experiences and emotions of father and son, as well as the whole family, teach us to live without masks, but with deep authenticity. To tear down barriers in demonstrating who we really are, who we really are, despite our human weaknesses, questions, or doubts. To have the willingness to let ourselves be molded by the great Potter – the Lord God Almighty.

I see Nassiff not only as a great friend and brother in Christ, but also an example of deep commitment to the Lord of Life: Jesus. In captivating simplicity, contagious joy, deep enthusiasm for life and people, he is that someone you would always want to have around.

These pages unfold a captivating narrative of how precious it is for us to realize just how dependent we are on the Lord of Life, his mercies, his teachings, and his actions, that transcend our understanding.

We are placed before a mirror and confronted with who we really are, how we understand, and deal and act in response to the circumstances presented to us.

This is an authentic manual of God's special work, in and through such a special human being: Rafael.

Odilar Francisco Bombardieri

Preface

I must confess that writing this preface was one of the most difficult tasks to come my way. I have rewritten it in my mind over and over because this is the story of a family I have learned to love and admire throughout the years.

I have known Nassiff since we were in seminary back in 1977, and more than that, I had the privilege of being close to his family when he joined the ministry alongside me at First Baptist Church of Curitiba.

I also had the privilege of witnessing many of the stories narrated here, and even if not being physically present, due to Nassiff's ministries in Canada and then in the U.S, I still continued to follow them from a distance.

Perhaps the unique mark of this family can be described as un-

conditional love. Something you learn altruistically, and often, in the midst of tears.

This book makes it clear that this was never a perfect family, for surely there is no such thing under the sun. But it also reveals a family that has tried to learn, amid struggles and suffering, to have unconditional love for one another and for the people to whom they minister.

Although the book is written as a memorial to Rafael's blessed presence among them, it is impossible not to notice along these pages how each member of this family developed this unconditional love in a singular way. Nivaldo, Lucia, Camila, Rafael, and Bruna; each and every one, in a unique and special way, are the targets as well as the givers of this love, in the most intense and various forms.

As you read through the pages, you will be challenged to learn how to find joy amid life's challenges. A joy which is this family's predominant mark. Not a stoic joy, or joy that is disconnected from reality as an escape. No! An elaborate joy, which does not deny the struggles, which is not cowardly. The kind that seeks in God answers that cannot always be found in this earthly dimension, but nevertheless, in order not to lose its integrity, always returns to the throne of grace. And what I have realized is that the answer from the throne has been unconditional love that is experienced and shared between them, and through them, it is shared with us.

In this sense, Rafael was certainly an angel in this house. But as I see it, the Nassiff family household is inhabited by angels, people who have learned to love and to live love for the glory of God.

Once again I say: not that they are perfect! They are human, experiencing ups and downs, even in their faith, but who still, after all, reveal unconditional love.

I am sure that reading this book will make you laugh and cry, but above all, it will challenge you to love.

Rev. Paschoal Piragine Jr.
Senior Pastor
First Baptist Curitiba
Paraná/Brazil

Introduction

This is an attempt to tell the life story of one of the most striking human beings I have ever met. A person full of love, passion, involvement with people, life, music, and good food. The only human being that I knew who was unable of doing any kind of evil to anyone. He would never be able to hurt anyone. In this world, Rafael was the true expression of a human being. He was a living example to humanity of what it means to be human.

I believe that the Holy Scriptures refer to holiness as the yearning to become human again. Being human is "being" the story of the first couple in the Bible: people who lived for each other and for God.

It seems to me that this is the task of the incarnate Christ when referred to in the Scriptures as the "second Adam." To be a "spiritual being" on this earth means being "absolutely human." You may also agree with me that the sense of humanity is being lost in (and from) humans. What have we become?

Rafael was the living proof that being human is possible. If I can, I will spend the rest of my days trying to remind myself of the most spectacular human with whom I lived. The most beautiful being our home, our church, and our community, had the privilege to see, feel, and love. We were all targets of his unconditional, unrestrained, indiscriminate, extravagant, and unstoppable love.

In the first few parts of this narrative, I allowed myself to expose my heart, my mind, my guts, living the pain of my loss. From April 21, 2017, to May 2, 2017, I lived the most horrendous days of my life. My heart was cruelly torn apart. My soul was confused, struck with such violence that produced unimaginable pain (which today seems to be eternal). My mind was (and still is) intoxicated by the shock, for it was subjected to a "double dose" of the bitterest drink of all. My body staggered (and still does) from dizziness, stunned, confused, with no direction. During that time, everything around me moved in slow motion. My vision was blurry. My senses were erased because I could not hear, nor could I see or taste, or smell anything or anyone. I didn't know why I was alive – or even if what I have now can be referred to as being alive.

From chapter 5 and on, I will share my conversations with God as I agonized before him, asking Him for an intervention of healing, which never came.

During the days in the hospital, I saw myself on the same boat as the disciples, in the midst of a storm, almost sinking, as Jesus slept peacefully. Jesus seemed indifferent to danger. The disciples shouted and Jesus awoke, calming the storm. Oh, how I screamed for Jesus to wake up in the boat of my son's life. I cried, and I cried, and I begged. It was no use! Jesus let the boat be consumed by the storm, sinking with my son. The sovereignty of the Lord means he can decide whom to deliver, whom to save, whom to heal. I cheerfully celebrate each time the Lord performs a miracle. However, since those days, I can't help but think, "Wow, He knows how to work miracles! Why didn't he do it for my son? I wonder why. Lord, will You let me know some day?"

The purpose of writing this book was not to offer consolation to those who have lost a child (and if this happens, I will be happy and grateful to God), but to show that each person reacts differently to their pain. Each life story is different and unique.

When I read A Grief Observed, by C.S. Lewis, I was encouraged to expose my pain as well.

Without any pretense, in my search for miracles, which never happened (at least not in the way I preferred). I have been agonizing before the Father. I still find myself having mixed emotions, with depressive peaks filled with hate and anger, intertwined with times of hope.

As King David once said (2 Samuel 12:33), at the news of his son's death, I also know (though I am not conformed) that my son will no longer return to me. But one day I will go to him. However, my wish is for counselors (professionals or nonprofessionals) to find in this narrative the help to understand that someone's pain is incomprehensible to everyone on the outside.

Each person has the right to express their pain, with all the feelings that this pain causes. May we at least be patient with those who suffer, understanding the uniqueness of each person avoiding the standard of "one size fits all."

I have avoided and still avoid using words and phrases such as "overcoming pain," "being restored from pain," "how to heal from pain." When I come across such expressions, I reject them immediately. My pain is mine alone, it is unequalled. So is everyone else's.

For me, there has never been a greater pain, more sharp or causing as much confusion of feelings as the pain of losing a son.

THE BEGINNING OF THE JOURNEY

1. RAFAEL'S LIFE, AN ANGEL *dressed* AS A HUMAN

On September 20, 1985, our second child, Rafael, was born. We already had our firstborn daughter, Camila. The Lord also blessed us with another daughter, our youngest, Bruna.

Rafael was born on a Friday night. The following morning, Lucia (my wife) called me from the hospital at 7 a.m. Camila and I were still asleep. Lucia said, "Honey, the baby looks strange, he's having difficulties nursing and looks so purple." To which I replied: "Honey, it's okay, that's normal." I did not understand a thing at all, did I? It was only an answer from a husband who did not know what to say. Then I said, "Has the doctor stopped by your room yet? Call him." Two hours went by and Lucia called again: "Honey, you need to come here." And she began to cry. "Hurry up! The doctor said that our son is a Mongoloid "- an expression used 30 or 40 years ago, which is strongly condemned nowadays. The pediatrician went to Lucia's room, which she shared with another patient. But the doctor did not speak to Lucia, just the other patient. As the doctor was leaving, Lucia asked about our son. The doctor simply responded, "Ahhh, your son is a Mongoloid. Ask your husband to talk to me." She left the room without giving any further explanation. Imagine the impact!

I took Camila, who was almost 4 years old, and walked a little over half a mile to my brother-in-law's to ask him if I could borrow his car. When I gave him the news, using the same term the doctor had said, Lucia's sister began to scream.

Upon arriving, I met Lucia crying frantically. Our hearts, souls, and minds were flooded with questions, fear, and confusion. After all, what or who was a mongoloid? A thing? A “non-human”? Would he talk? Would he walk? Would he survive? What did it all mean?

Back in those days there was no such thing as the Internet. We went to the library in hopes of finding something that would explain what was happening to us.

Finally, after about a month filled with anguish and fear, we were brought to APAE (Association of Parents and Friends of Special Needs Children) in São Paulo, Brazil. There, we were once again shocked by the horrifying reality we faced: various syndromes, types of disabilities and limitations to young children. Hundreds of families were in pain and despair, just like Lucia and I. However, it was at APAE where we were welcomed, cared for, and treated. We owe so much to that place!

LIVING THE FIRST MOURNING

When Lucia was pregnant, we were expecting an "ideal" child, one we idealized and dreamed of. We had always wanted a boy. I wanted to take him to soccer matches and watch him grow. I dreamed of him graduating college, getting married, and giving me grandchildren. However, when Rafael was born, we were told he was a “mongoloid.” We then had to “bury” the ideal son and bring our real son home. The “ideal” son had to be mourned. It lasted about this 3 years. The real son had to be taken home, loved, and taken care of, while we were completely clueless about his possibilities and his future. We knew nothing! Our perspective of what lied ahead was in the dark.

However, we instantly realized that along with Rafael a new love had been born. As great and infinite as the love we have for our daughters. It was a different, special kind of love. And what a love, what an overwhelming passion, what a feeling of protection and affection was born inside of us on September 20, 1985.

It would be the start of a bleak season regarding the future. We cried not for feeling rejected or being non-conformed (we could not get over the “death” of our “ideal” son), but because we didn't have any source of information – like we do today – about our son's condition, who he was or what he had. We were scared for him, that he might suffer. What should we do? How should we raise him? How should we educate him? How could we protect him? Everything was frightening at the time. As the months and years went by, we were able to realize how God had been guiding us through paths that led to great joy and satisfaction. We were learning just how much God had blessed us, by specifically choosing us to be parents to the angel named Rafael.

CHOOSING THE NAME RAFAEL

Lucia picked out his name. Out of nowhere she said, "I like Rafael." I ran to the registry and told them the name of our son, our angel in a human body: RAFAEL.

Rafael is a biblical name. Rafa-el. Rafa: healed, or used to heal. El: God. The one healed by God, or the one God uses to heal. The Rafael from the bible was the gatekeeper to the temple. With this information in hand, I asked my wife what she preferred: that God would heal our son Rafael, or that He would use our Rafael as the temple's "gatekeeper." My wife, holding our Rafa in her arms, looking at him with tears in her eyes, said "I want our son the way God created him and gave him to us. I choose gatekeeper." God honored Lucia's choice.

Dozens of people were brought to Jesus through

Rafael because of his friendly ways, his love, and care for everyone. Rafa – which is how we lovingly called him – loved going out to eat. It was his favorite thing to do, and mine too. Whenever we were at a restaurant, he would always ask the waiter, "What's your name?" After getting an answer, he would say, "Very nice to meet you, my name is Rafael. Jesus loves you." Then he would go on, "This is my dad, he's a pastor." Then he would turn to me and say "Daddy..." He was a true gatekeeper! He would "bring people in," and then expect me to do my part. Because of this great example, we still write on the receipt, after every meal. "Jesus loves you!" – and include a generous tip.

THE FIRST CHALLENGES

Rafa needs to smile, Yes, smile. Smiling would be a sign that his syndrome was at a smaller degree – there are different degrees: light, moderate, critical, and severe. We would do every funny thing we could think of in front of that baby. And then one day, he finally smiled – or so we thought. We jumped and cried with happiness and gratefulness.

Children with Down Syndrome are born with generalized hypotonia, which is a generalized muscle flaccidity. Therefore, they need physical therapy from the time they are babies. Every day, he went through hours and hours of stimulation to keep his head from flopping, to enable him to use his hands and fingers, and to learn how to walk. Lucia would kneel behind him, holding him by his waist, and push him to make him walk, as if he were a doll. This would be our routine for two hours in the morning and two hours in the afternoon, every day, for two years. Everything Rafa knew had to be taught to him. He didn't just learn things naturally. Smiling, waving goodbye, sitting, walking, saying "excuse me," "please," and "thank you." Being respectful, learning boundaries, praying, and trusting God.

Everything was learned by setting the example. It was a tough discipleship. If I needed a napkin, I couldn't just say, "Lu, can you throw me a napkin?" Because if she did throw it, Rafa would throw anything that was asked of him. I needed to be constantly aware, and this is how I needed to ask for a napkin: "Lucia, could you please pass me the napkin?" And she would answer "Of course, here it is! Love you!" It was learning by copying a model. It was painful, difficult, but it was the only way. After all, children observe, act on, and repeat the examples they have.

An environment at home is perpetuated into its children until the fifth generation. Would this be something to think about for our country Brazil? We are the product, or byproduct, of the last five generations! We cannot change the past, but we can certainly change our future if only we become better role models at home. Simply punishing those who are corrupt isn't going to solve the problem, as long as our own corruptions don't end at home, where our children are learning from our own values (which aren't worth much, maybe nothing at all).

The first time Rafa was used as the "gatekeeper to the temple," was precisely at APAE. When we were interviewed by the social worker, among other things we were asked, "What do you do for a living?" I answered, "I'm a Baptist pastor." To which she asked, "How do your religious beliefs interpret what has happened in your family, with the arrival of your son?" I said, "Rafael is a blessing in our lives, he is the result of divine creation." The social worker was shocked. She said, "We work with a protestant couple who say their little daughter, who also has Down syndrome, is a target for the Devil's work. They are praying that God may 'set her free' so that they won't have to bring her to APAE." We reached out to the couple with a lot of love (because of Rafa) and we were able to help them comprehend what was happening to them through scripture. With that, they were able to accept their daughter as a special gift from God and took very good care of her. This was the first time God used our angel, Rafa.

THE FIRST YEARS

From the time Rafa was 4 until he was about 12 or 13 years old, he was unstoppable. He would run away from home. He had no perception of danger. Doors and windows had to be locked, chained up, and keys had to be hidden. Nothing ever stayed in place; he would knock over chairs, tables, bookshelves, TV's, etc. He would throw things out of the window, and everything would come crashing down. In a matter of seconds, he would run across a busy street. We would hear cars braking and dodging him and horns going crazy. One day, when we lived in Uruguay, Rafa ran away and crossed an intersection where the South American Cycling Competition was taking place. We watched cyclists piling on top of each other as they collided in an attempt to steer clear from him. And what about Rafa? Safely on the other side of the road, laughing and enjoying every second of it. It was extremely embarrassing. Whenever we would arrive at someone's house, we would notice that there had been strategic changes to the décor, that is, no pictures hanging from the walls, no flower vases, nothing! Everything had been removed in anticipation of Rafa.

It was very hard to accept that Rafa was never welcomed in regular schools. One allegation was that parents of "normal" children were afraid their

children would copy Rafa's behavior. Another was that a special needs child wasn't very appealing to the eye, so parents feared that their children would feel traumatized and emotionally scared. Their children needed to be sheltered from "human aberrations."

What was even harder for us was the time when he was denied access to a school for special needs children. With each rejection, we felt rejected too. Would the way the world viewed kids like him ever change? Would they ever be more loved, accepted, and understood? These were tough questions that caused anguish and uneasiness. The path was dark, and we needed to take the next step in blindness and uncertainty. Would they ever be accepted? Or at least tolerated and not discriminated against?

2. LESSONS FROM AN Angel

Throughout his whole life, Rafael was an angel God used to teach us very important lessons. These lessons humbled us at times, other times made us happy. Regardless, they always made us better humans.

In the following chapter, I will mention some of the precious lessons we were taught, day after day, through the angel that lived in our home.

ADJUSTSMENTS IN OUR MARRIAGE

We thank God for having a faith that taught us how much our God was in control of our situation. Even if we were still blindly stumbling forward in the new paths imposed upon us, and even though we were still very young and lacking the information which is available today about Down Syndrome, we realized that the grace of God sustained us.

However, adjustments were needed and implemented. We realized that being new parents of a special child brought us significant emotional frailty. By the grace of God, all of that united us much more. Very early on we began to learn that the storms of life, no matter where they came from or originated, could unite us even more, or separate us, destroying our marriage. We have learned that all the storms of life, all the critical aspects of existence, all these experiences, would bring about radical and lifelong changes. Whether these changes would be for better or for worse, that would depend on us alone. Furthermore, it would depend on each one individually. As a couple, you can only change one person: yourself. Lucia and I decided to come together even more, love one another, and pay more attention to the needs (especially the emotional ones) of each other.

Since then, we credit a lot to Rafa in the sense that he taught us that the challenges of life have always united us more and have always produced a greater degree of complicity. They produced more passion, love, and unity. No, it was not an easy road. It was painful and complicated. It was and has been a constant learning process.

Rafa has taught us that the most excellent way was, and always will be, the way of love. Throughout our lives, we have learned that forgiveness would have to be generous and overcoming. That is, to always forgive more often than being hurt. Our passions had to be renewed by a premeditated stance of breaking free of the routine rut, reinventing pleasures, innovating relationships, affections, and caresses. Our angel taught us that throughout our lives.

LETTING OUR DAUGHTERS COME IN SECOND PLACE

During his early years, Rafael drained us in such a way that we could rarely give due attention to our daughters. Our youngest one was tremendously impacted by our "absence."

Our daughters were, are, and always will be, loved with an infinite love, exclusively to them.

In those stormy years, due to Rafael's special situation, our youngest daughter felt rejected. From the age of three she was absolutely certain that she would be abandoned in a corner of the city. For her, the truth was that we did not love her and that we were planning to leave her alone in a distant place so that she would never be able to return home.

She was quiet. She never complained or cried. She looked like an angel; and she was. She was hurt. Deeply wounded by our distraction and emotional exhaustion.

One day she began to lose her hair, eyelashes and

eyebrows. At last, her body had managed to pull off a trick, forcing everyone to notice it.

When a child does not feel loved, he or she seeks to replace the missing love for attention. She had accomplished that. Now, people would not only ask, "How's Rafael?" But they also added: "Wow, what happened to Bruna?"

We prayed and cried a lot. With a sense of guilt, of having failed as parents. We blamed ourselves each day for having "abandoned" our little baby. With much treatment (spiritual and psychological) we managed to overcome those years. Bruna's hair, eyebrows and eyelashes grew back.

The hard lesson we learned was that there also existed other members in the family of a special needs person. No one can be left behind. All members of a family should receive care, protection, attention, courage, love, and quality time, equally. Such a task is very difficult, but it must be fulfilled.

TO FROM "MARICON" TO "SUPERMACHO"

Our family lived in Uruguay from 1989 to 1991 for missionary training. It was meant to be a multicultural training experience and implementation of a new church. We had the great opportunity of working with such wonderful and brave people. We lived there with a group of Brazilians who were also in training. Every afternoon, we would walk the streets to connect with the locals, learn the language, and serve those special people.

At the time we arrived, our daughter Camila was 7, Rafael was 3, and Bruna was only a few months old.

We didn't have a telephone at home (cellphones didn't exist), or a computer. Every morning I would go out to run errands with Rafael strapped to a stroller.

Since Rafa was hyperactive at the time and would knock things off the shelves at the market and at the stores, and because he would sometimes run away, I had no choice but to have him in the stroller. I would run down the sidewalks pushing him and he would laugh. He loved our outings. However, I did notice that the "gauchos", which were men that wore boots, carried knives in their big leather belts, and drank hot matcha in front of bars, would look at me and talk amongst them. I noticed, that day after day those men would stare at me. One day, I decided to share this with a local friend. He asked, "When you push the stroller, is your wife by your side?" I said, "No, it's just me and Rafa." He looked shocked and said, "Don't ever do that again!" I asked why but he didn't want to tell me the reason. I insisted, and he finally said, "It's just that here in Uruguay, the only men who push their kids around in their strollers without their wives are considered "MARICONES" (a demeaning way of calling someone gay). For that context, at that time, in a male chauvinist culture, where men loved to display their "manliness," I was being talked about as the Brazilian missionary "maricon." In other words, aside from the bad impression I was leaving (according to that time), they would never accept the Gospel coming from me. They would associate my words with my "way" of being and living. So, I asked my friend what I should do. I couldn't just leave him at home, I had to help my wife. He said, "Carry him in your arms or shoulders." I said, "Are you serious?" and he nodded yes.

For the next few days I would carry Rafa on my shoulders, everywhere we went, when it was just the two of us. I noticed that the "gauchos" still stared and whispered to each other. I went after my friend again and told him that nothing had changed to which he replied, "Don't worry, everything is okay now."

One or two months later, a lady knocked on our door. She introduced herself as the principal of a school for special needs children in the city of Florida, Uruguay.

We invited her in and she asked us, "Why do you carry your son on your shoulders when you walk around town?" I answered her question with another question, "Is it wrong to do so?" She said, "You're the talk of the town. The gauchos can't stop talking about you." She added, "In our culture, masculinity is worshipped.

Whenever one of these men has a child who happens to be mentally or physically handicapped, their masculinity is considered to have been put at risk, because he created something that is 'defective.' Which in turn, means he's not fully a man.

Because of it, when they become a father of special needs child, they hide these children at home, don't take them to school, and don't even let the school bus stop in front of their houses. If a friend asks them about the child, he runs the risk of being stabbed because the father might interpret the question as someone mistrusting his masculinity. Because of this way of thinking, we haven't been able to give these children a better quality of life. You, however, have been carrying your son on your shoulders every day and these men are calling you 'super macho,' someone who is not ashamed of his son and who is not afraid of having his masculinity questioned. That is why I'm here. Would you be able to help us? You could go to these parents' houses and talk to them. Convince them to bring their children to the school where we can help them."

Isn't it incredible how a simple act can have you called a "maricon." And how just by asking a local, you can change the way you are viewed in a small town (at that time, Florida had about 25,000 people). From "maricon" to "super macho," and a request to help families transform their children's futures. It was our angel Rafael teaching us another lesson.

TO EACH HIS OWN

One day I was walking past the bathroom. The door was cracked open and I saw Rafa sitting on the toilet. I asked, "Rafito (which is how I called him), do you need help wiping your behind?" To which he answered, "Palinho, everyone should take care of their own behinds!"

It was our angel teaching us not to intrude in other people's lives and each one should answer for him/herself. Rafa always tried to be independent and never intruded in other people's lives.

He had an intense love for people, life, his friends, and parties.

He was extremely obedient. Never invaded other people's business. He would always ask permission to talk by raising his hand. He knew how to be in his own space where he was king and where others couldn't invade. He never disrespected another person's personal space.

How often do we see people intruding on other people lives! Rafa taught us that just taking care of ourselves was enough. Why snoop around somewhere you have not been invited to?

Rafa liked to live his way. He never stereotyped anyone. When we went to Walmart we would always come across the same customers: those people that would dress in a way we would only see at Walmart. People in their PJ's, adults wearing costumes and exotic outfits. Rafa never noticed these "differences." Only when he saw a pretty girl would he elbow me and ask, "What do you think, dad?"

Rafa lived his life with joy. All that mattered was that he could be himself, be happy, and allow others to be happy in their own way. "Dad, everyone should take care of their own behind."

SMOKING CAUSES ERECTILE DYSFUNCTION

One time, Rafa and I went to the arena to watch our soccer team, Atletico, play a match against Internacional. It was an important soccer match in the Brazilian Championship and our team was losing 2x0 in the first half. Everyone was angry.

A guy sitting next to me was smoking. He would light one cigarette after another, the whole time we had been there. Rafa, sitting on the other side of me kept saying, "Palinho, that guy is smoking cigarettes." To which I would reply, "Rafito, be quiet, let him smoke." Then he would poke me again and say, “He’s smoking!” I was afraid the guy would punch me so I said to Rafa, “Be quiet! Leave him alone. If he hits me, I’ll hit you.” But he wouldn’t stop. He kept repeating, “Dad, he’s smoking!” So, I said, “If you don’t stop talking about it, you’re not getting any food during halftime.” I thought that had worked, but no. He leaned over my lap and poked the guy next to me and said, “Hey! Smoking causes erectile dysfunction!” I closed my eyes and waited for the punch. But to my surprise, the guy started laughing hysterically. As a result, my faith and courage returned, and I turned to him and said, “My bad, pal. The boy is a Christian and is worried about your health.”

In Brazil, cigarette advertisements always contain a phrase from the Department of Health warning about, warning about the dangers of smoking. I do not know why, but Rafael remembered the one that warned about the possibility of sexual impotence for smokers. Rafa did not intrude on anyone's life and lifestyle. But when he saw someone at risk, he would move toward that person to alert or help in some way. His level of sensitivity to the suffering of others was impressive. Any human being was the object of his love, protection, care, and affection. He loved life, loved living, and would do anything to help those he believed to be in danger, pain, or anguish.

SAMBA PARTY AT MY HOUSE

Between 1995 and 2000, I worked as one of the pastors at First Baptist Church of Curitiba.

On one occasion, we had one of those services that really impacted our lives. God's presence there was wonderful. The worship minister at the time (the late Pastor Marcilio de Oliveira), invited Rafael to sing the last song of the night with him. All of a sudden, Rafa pulled Marcilio close to him and asked if he could make an announcement to the church. Pastor Marcilio gave him the microphone and Rafa said, "Hey everyone! Everyone is invited to come to my house tomorrow for a big samba party!" The whole church was laughing. Rafa ruined the service. I almost lost my job. Can you imagine? The pastor's son inviting the church, right after Sunday's service, to a party with samba.

Rafael loved music and didn't see the difference between worldly or gospel music. To him, everything was "sacred." To him, all sounds, all colors, all styles, had their origin in God. Therefore, they should be experienced. The church service was as sacred and entertaining as a round of samba with his friends (and the whole church) together with him, celebrating life. Songs, celebrations, people dancing, people toasting, that was "heaven" for our Rafa. He knew how to dance all rhythms, to sing every style of music, to celebrate every minute of his life, always surrounded by friends. "Tomorrow," my beloved son, we will be home with you, our eternal home, throwing great parties, filled with every sound, every instrument, with all our friends, for our God. Son, I have already started my trip home, where you now live.

PASTOR RAFAEL

There was a time (around 2009), when Rafa began to tell me he wanted to be a pastor. I never really took this seriously, so I basically ignored him. Rafa liked everything I did, so it was normal for him to say that.

What was interesting was that Rafa had the same care, passion, and compassion for people and he liked to pray, visit the sick, and leave messages to those going through a difficult time. Since I didn't heed to his prompting, he picked up the phone and without my knowledge, called our dear friend who was the director of Florida Christian University. He left a message with the receptionist saying that he wanted to study theology, so he could become a pastor. The school secretary advised the director who, impressed by his request, called him and gave him a one-year scholarship. Rafa went to class with me for a year. He was a "special student." After a year, FCU kindly allowed him to graduate, where he received the diploma of "Special Pastor." He was amazed with his scholarship, his diploma, and his graduation party.

A few days later, he asked me if he was already a pastor. To which I replied: "Come on! You have to wait a little longer."

One day he heard me telling my wife that I was going to a council of a candidate for the pastorate. He asked me: "Palinho, what is that?" When I explained, he immediately asked when it would be his turn. I did not take any action. A month later, I learned from a deacon of my church that he had called all the church's small groups to announce his examining council, as a candidate for the pastorate. The people of the church had a party and "forced" me to "test" Rafa. We asked him three questions: "Rafael do you love Jesus? Take care of His sheep. Rafael, do you love Jesus? Take care of His sheep. Rafael, do you love Jesus? Take care of His sheep!"

Thus, in 2011, Rafa was recognized by the church as "Special Pastor."

In the year 2014, Pastor David Uth, senior pastor at First Baptist Church in Orlando, introduced him to the pastors of the church as Pastor Rafael. Not only did he enjoy it, but he really saw himself as a caretaker of people.

He joined me in dozens of pastoral visits in homes, hospitals, and clinics. He prayed for the sick. He prayed intensely for pregnant women. He knew their names, the baby's name, and when the baby was due. Of course, he would always go to the hospital to visit Mom and the baby.

He called everyone on their birthdays, he'd never forget anyone. He was my partner, truly a super-special shepherd. Oh, how I miss him.

During the service celebrating his life, Pastor David Uth said: "When we invited Nassiff to be the pastor of the Brazilians among us, we did not know Rafael. If we had known him, we would certainly have invited him, instead."

YOU DON'T LIKE IT, BUT I DO

From time to time Rafael would come up with new habits and likings.

He always loved music (samba, funk, country, bossa nova, soundtracks to soap operas, rock, gospel, etc.). It was unbelievable to see how he knew every name to every song and everyone who sang it. He loved restaurants and going out to eat. From junk food to the more sophisticated ones. He liked watching wrestling, WWE in particular. He liked soccer and would cheer for a different team every week. He was always in love with actresses from the current Brazilian soap opera. From time to time he'd come up with a new interest or a new habit and I would comment, "Rafa, that song is terrible," or "that show is no good," to which he would always reply "Daddy, you don't like it, but I do!"

That's it, that was the lesson. Each of us has the right to like whatever we want.

My likes and dislikes won't always be the same as yours. Your likes and dislikes won't always be the same as mine. You have every right to like, appreciate, and experience whatever you want. Even if I don't have the same interests. Do you know why? Because it's your life, it's what makes you feel good, it's what brings you happiness and joy.

Just don't forget that your absolute right to choose also means I have my absolute right to choose. Choose how you want to be happy, go in peace, and don't try to tell me how to be happy. My interests, my passions, my habits, are all mine. If you don't like them, that's okay!

I learned from Rafa that oftentimes what parents dream for their children are their own dreams, not their children's. My children will do this or that, they will study this or that. When parents say that, it's the realization of the parents' dreams and happiness, but not necessarily of the child's.

To make my son happy was to provide what gave him pleasure, joy, laughter, passion, and security. Rafa taught me that nothing can bring such happiness to a father than to see his children happy. Watching him laugh out loud, even if for that to happen I had to pretend to have tripped or banged my head on the door, it was a moment of feeling heaven with him. Watching him laugh hysterically and roll on the floor, was the happiest thing in the world for me. Of course, we as parents should always guide our children to what is best. Ultimately, our children's happiness will always be their happiness and never a forced projection of our happiness, or our understanding of what happiness may be into their lives, "Palinho, you do not like it, but don't it!"

Oh, how I miss hearing you sing your songs, hearing your steps through the house. You standing at the door in our room every night, to ask me and Lucia, "Are you going to have sex tonight?" and then laugh loudly. How I miss hearing the living room door open and seeing him sweating, after his physical exercises to the sound of his Pentecostal singers. How I miss his company in my car, where he loved to be, feeling the wind on our faces and his left hand resting on mine.

DON'T BE UPSET, DADDY

Sometimes, I would get home very tired and he would start chatting or singing very loudly. I would say, "Rafa, daddy is not well. I'm tired and stressed. Give me a few minutes, will you?" To that, he would sit next to me, caress my head with his hand and say, "Daddy, don't be stressed out! Here's what you should do: Take mom out to a nice restaurant, have a romantic dinner with her. Then take her to a hotel, open a champagne bottle, take a bath with her and come back tomorrow, okay? You'll feel a lot better. What do you think?"

How did he come up with these ideas? I don't know. He would always try to find alternatives to make us feel better. He was always in search of joy and well-being for him and those around him. He wanted relationships filled with understanding and care. He had an inexplicable understanding of relationships. He could tell when people were suffering and always looked for ways of relief and alternatives for healing. He suffered with those who suffered and rejoiced with those who were happy. The angel Rafael was tireless and unstoppable, until he could find ways of healing, joy, and blessings in the lives of those around him.

NO LIMITS

Rafael knew how to be happy. He did not realize his limitations (did he even have any?). He always did what he liked to do. The definition of happiness was always his.

We soon learned that the "happiness" we project in our children is almost always "our" (personal) projection of happiness.

Many times, we wish for our children what we think would make them happy. At other times, we project onto our children what we ourselves failed to be or do. In a way, there is nothing wrong with that.

Of course, we always want our children to have more and better opportunities than we did. But the projection of our happiness on them is not always realistic. Every human being is unique. Each one, under the guidance, care, and protection of their parents, must find his way to happiness. Our Rafa knew exactly how to do that.

Another day, he decided that he would be a shepherd of souls. And he was! The most extraordinary shepherd of souls I've ever known. His passion for people, his intense fight to see people free from their pain, the way he prayed for other people, the way he sang his hymns to God, were second to none.

The other day, he decided he was an "event promoter." He told us that he worked for events. When he saw a poster of any of these events, he would spread the word to everyone. He was working.

After that, he approached me and said: "Palinho, I'm going to be a “potographer”! I replied: "Wow! Really, my son? And what is a “potographer”? " With a face of admiration and shock, because of my ignorance, he replied: “potographer” takes pictures of people, newborn babies, birthdays, weddings, etc. Get it?” On his birthday, a group of our friends got together and gifted him with a semi-professional camera. Rafa would take it everywhere, taking pictures of everything and everyone.

He was the “potographer” working happily, developing his skills with extreme satisfaction. Some photos were perfect. Some scenes were woven with a sensitivity to life that impressed us!

GOD SPOKE TO RAFA

We believe that Rafael had an ability to understand when God spoke to him.

He told me many times that he had heard the voice of the Lord in his heart. Certainly, he had a special communication with God. He was never wrong in his "predictions." Several times he would call our family in São Paulo, Brazil and say that he would go to a cousin's wedding, or spend Christmas and New Years there, or go to see a baby who had been born. It was amazing to see how things ended working out in a way to that everything would come out as he'd said.

I strongly believe that the Lord spoke to him that week about death. Two days after the surgery, he asked me: "Palinho, do you think I'm going to die?" I tried to tell him no. But turning his face away suddenly, he said to me: "Palinho, I don't want to talk about it now." And slept peacefully. When he awoke, neither he nor I touched the subject. In a way, that only he knew and understood, God communicated with him in a special way. He already knew that he would live in Heaven.

He taught me that my level of education or intellectuality often prevented me from "hearing" the Lord and from knowing the Lord. For many people, their intellectuality serves as artificial light that prevents them from seeing the sky dotted with trillions and trillions of stars.

If you turn off the lights in the city, you will see a sky like you've never seen. Often times our intellect works, in our hearts and minds, like these artificial lights, which hide the stars from the sky. He taught me that intellectual ability (especially of those who know only a little of something, and think they know everything) can disrupt their sensitivity to God. The Lord's power, glory and majesty goes unnoticed by us. He could hear, feel, and enter the presence of the Lord, as if he were transferred. He could hardly read, but understood divine truths with impressive depth.

SENSIBILITY AND A SENSE OF URGENCY

When a person was suffering, Rafael knew that the relief needed to be felt immediately. He had an incredible sensitivity to the suffering of others.

When I knew of someone who was ill, he prayed immediately, insisting me to visit the ill the same day. When it came from a person far away, he sent voice messages and songs with lyrics that always had everything to do with what they were going through.

Once, when I had a terrible migraine, I was caught up in the pain and dizziness while driving home. Lucia and Rafa were with me. Lucia wanted to drive, but I could not move. I drove home very slowly, locked behind the wheel like a statue. Rafa put his hand on my shoulder and kept saying: "Calm down, calm down, it will pass, it will pass." Everything around him lost its meaning, or his interest, because he was absolutely focused on helping me. On that occasion he sometimes talked to himself out loud: "Dude, when you get home, pray a lot for Palinho." When we got home, the migraine worsened. I could not get out of the car. I felt so much dizziness and extreme pain. I was screaming and groaning in agony. At that moment, Rafa said "Oh dude, you better start raising a prayer outcry now!" So, he did. Then, he'd visit me in my room every hour to ask if Jesus had healed me yet.cHe would kiss me and run his hand over my arm. Then, he would go back to his room and keep praying. It was a loud outcry. He asked Jesus to heal his dad. He would cry while he prayed. Then, just from hearing his cry, I would get out of bed and go to his room to tell him that I was feeling much better, just to calm him down. He fought with God. He fought hard for anyone in distress.

Rafael always had an attitude towards those who suffered that took him to act fast. He did not procrastinate in the face of anyone's suffering. He'd run to get help. He suffered with whomever was suffering.

On those occasions, we'd always question if he was, after all, only human. For he behaved like an angel who provided for everyone around him and kept them safe!

He had an indestructible and deep conviction that he could speak to God. Moreover, he had deep faith that the Lord heard, understood, and acted in response to his prayers.

Since he had such intimacy with the Lord, it seems that He

took him to spend the hours of eternity having the most pleasant conversations in the eternal abodes. Certainly, the angel Rafael is now being visited by the Father

RAFAEL LOVED WITH UNCONDITIONAL AND EXTRAVAGANT LOVE

He always knew how to love. He loved all people indiscriminately and unconditionally. He did not care who the person in front of him was. Any human being was the target of his love, indiscriminate, unconditional, and extravagant love.

He did not care about anyone's physical aspect. The way they dressed, whether they were short, tall, fat or skinny. For him, it made no difference the color of anyone's skin. He did not care what religion they belonged to, which soccer team they rooted for, or their sexual orientation. He embraced, was affectionate, and loved all people.

He taught me not to discriminate, not even to stereotype any human being. He taught me to love, hug, and kiss all people.

In the church that I pastor I hug and kiss everyone. That maybe the reason to why in every service that I preach there are many people from other religions, such as Catholics, Muslims, Jews, etc. When they come to our services, they tell me that the environment is safe, whole, and permeated with love.

I hug and kiss all my "sheep," whether they are women or men. The kiss is always followed by a: "God bless you." The hug is always strong and time-consuming.

Rafael taught us to hug so that through our arms we may give and receive healing to our emotions. He taught me that no one needs to change to be loved. We always love, without expectations. On the contrary, we do everything to love everyone. Because of this, we'd never speak badly of or criticize anyone in front of Rafael.

On many occasions he would say to me: " Palinho, I miss so and so a lot! " And I squirmed inside because that person was someone who hurt us a lot at some point in our lives. But Rafa never knew anything about what they did to us. When we speak badly of someone, we murder the morals and the personality of whom we speak in the heart of the one to whom we speak. We did not have the courage (and Rafa did not deserve it) to do this to his pure heart. Thus, he loved even those we never wanted to see, or hear from, again.

BE CAREFUL WITH WHAT YOU SAY, DADDY

One day, Lucia and I were on our way to pick him up from his friends' house, after he spent the day with them. On the way there, we talked about a young woman from our church who sang beautifully. She had an impressive voice and sang with a passion for God that was contagious.

Sometimes when we want to praise someone very much we sarcastically say: "That girl can't sing at all, huh?" But of course what we mean is the exact opposite. Right at that moment Rafa entered the car and heard us talking about that young woman. As he had always believed in everything I taught him, he was sure I meant what I said, in the most literal sense, and at the first opportunity he had, he said to the young woman, "Did you know that my father does not like the way you sing?" That young woman was devastated! It was not easy to explain what had happened. Thank God, she was our close friend and understood. But we learned that what parents say in the car, at home, in front of their children, or anywhere, they listen because they are super attuned to, trust in, and believe their parents. Because of this, Rafa only heard good things about everyone, even those we did not like.

He taught us that we are the masters of the words we keep and slaves of the ones we say out loud.

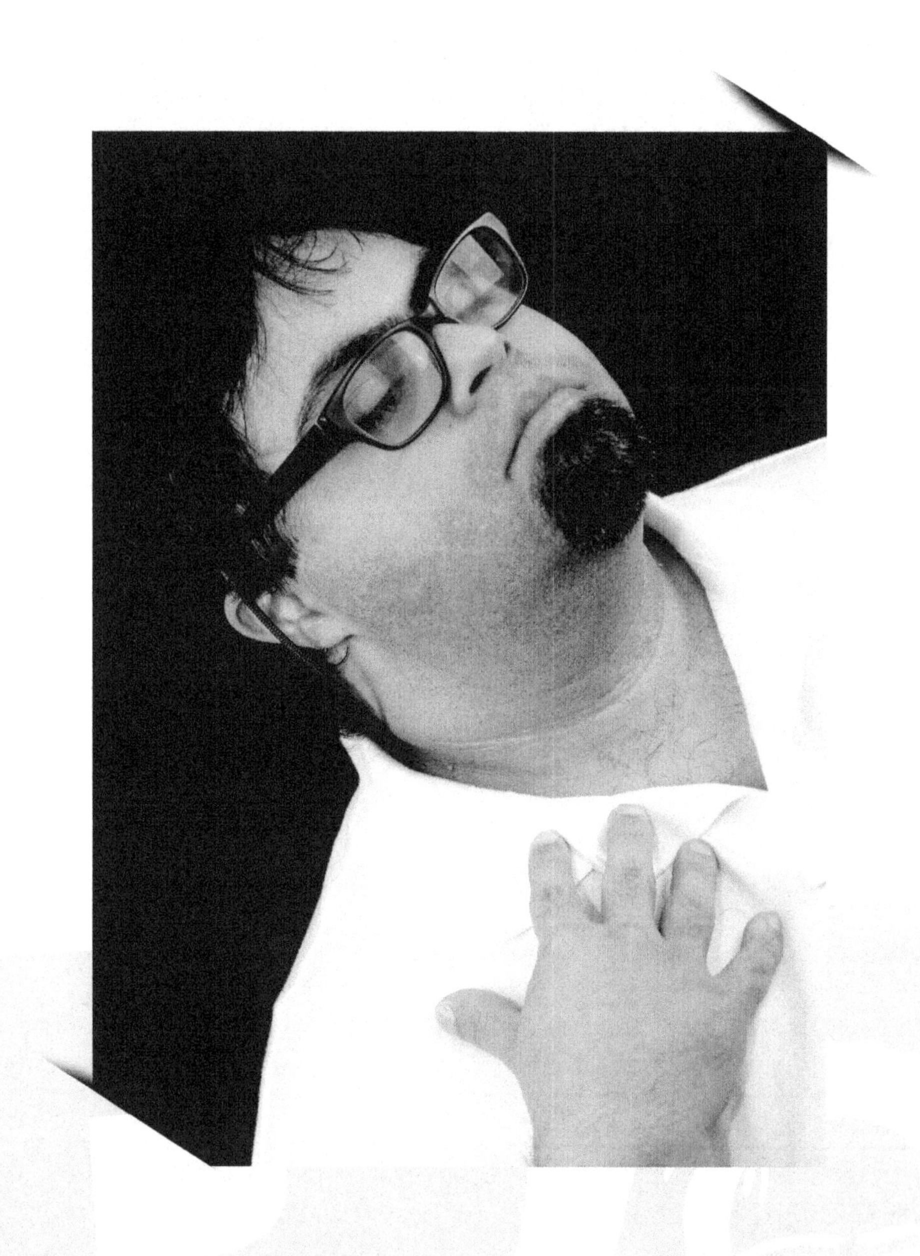

3. HIS LAST YEARS IN *Orlando*

My life as a pastor led us to live in many places. We lived in São Paulo and Curitiba, Brazil, Florida, Uruguay, Boston, Massachusetts, and currently Orlando, Florida.

In 2002, we moved to Boston, where I pastored a Brazilian Baptist church. It was an enriching experience and also very difficult (during our last years in that region). The church had grown and then declined sharply during the 2008 U.S. economic crisis.

It was a time of much misunderstanding, accusations, crying, and depression. We lost our home and later left the church, for we understood that the same people who were used by God to invite us were now being used again to plan our departure. We prayed a lot.

Before making the decision to leave, I prayed in the church for six months. Every day at 5 in the morning, on sunny or snowy days, I would bend my knees at the foot of the pulpit of that church and weep until 7 in the morning. Then I would get up and go to a part-time job outside the church.

The heavens were closed. Until one day the Lord signaled to me, without doubt and with some confirmations, that it would be time to surrender the position of pastoring that church. We left in pain because we loved those people.

Under these new circumstances, I went to work in a clinic that cared for children with emotional disorders. There, I gained tremendous experience in psychotherapeutic treatment, and I was able to help some people. Again, God was using all of this to signal the next change in our lives.

One day, God began to do something within our hearts. Not too long after that, I was invited to lead a department of an American church in the city of Orlando. I had been accepted to be the pastor of Brazilians within the American church.

In Orlando, Rafael had the best years of his life. He had grown and made hundreds and hundreds of friends. He learned to broadcast his physical exercises, his time of worship, and his joy live through Facebook. He'd send his audio messages and videos to everyone on their birthdays. Sometimes, he'd sing with the church's worship team. He was happy. Very happy. Everyone around him could feel his joy.

He lived abundantly in Orlando and in his church. He danced, laughed, worshipped, served, and loved people. However, we did not know that in Orlando we would live the most painful days of our lives, when our angel began his journey toward his eternal abode.

As C.S Lewis once said, "Now, the sky over this city covers my head with the remembrance of my beloved." Every corner, building, sidewalk, restaurant, park, reminds me of the best years of our son's life. They remind me, with everlasting gratitude to God, for the best 31 years and 7 months of our lives!

Somehow, God's comfort and blessings are as strong and extravagant as the longing for our son. This longing which causes sharp, violent pain. At the same time, the consolation that comes from the Lord is, in turn, deep, strong, and comforting.

When the longing tries to paralyze us, the consolations that come from the Holy Spirit of the Lord push us to live, to love, and to dream. Somewhere in my heart I perceive, in a faint but real way, a flame that begins to warm my soul. Proclaiming, still as whispers, that the coexistence with this pain will be bearable. That my eyes will still cry with more tears of gratitude and not just pain.

How do I define myself today? Like a sad person! Before I could define myself as a happy person, who sometimes felt sad. Today, essentially, I define myself as a sad person. With some hope of finding some joys in this existential world, not chosen by me.

4. IN THE VALLEY OF *the shadow* OF DEATH

GOING TO LIVE WITH THE FATHER

In December 2016, Rafa was infected by a ferocious bacterium that took him to the hospital. After 2 months of battle, we managed to free him from that terrible disease.

After the healing phase, he was to undergo reconstructive surgery of the genital area. So after much discussion with the doctors, family, and lots of prayer, we decided to go through with the surgery.

On April 18, 2017, we took him to the hospital.

Rafa did well in surgery. It lasted 8 long hours in the operating room. Days later he was free to go home. However, while still in the hospital, he suffered a thrombosis that caused a pulmonary embolism, leading him to a respiratory arrest, on April 21 at 7:30 a.m. in my arms.

Our son's last words were, "Daddy, daddy, my head hurts, I'm afraid. Help me Palinho, help me." Then he lost his ability to speak, so he would hit me with all his might on my chest, crying out for help. Then, with a hideous expression of dread, he stopped breathing.

I never heard his voice again. It was the most horrific morning, the most desperate we had ever felt in our lives.

Those moments were embedded in our minds. Impossible to forget, even for a few minutes. It was terrifying.

His cries, calling for help, still ring in my mind; all the time. The room was filled with doctors trying to revive him. He was intubated and taken to the Intensive Care Unit. They had to remove the clots from his lungs and from the left side of his heart. During the process, his heart stopped for half an hour. This caused immense damage to his brain and we knew that we could not have him back.

In the days that followed, he had pneumonia, appendicitis, and sinusitis. Later, bacteria began to take over his body. Due to all the movement in the attempt to resuscitate him, the stitches from the surgery burst open in a horrific way. He was put into deep sedation and the struggle for his life began.

MY CONVERSATIONS WITH GOD

During those days, I sought the Lord in my prayers, and He showed me passages from the Bible. Those texts were so different before my eyes flooded with tears and my heart dressed in deep pain, that the more I read them, the more intense the pain felt.

Dr. Henrik Fexeus, in his book "The Art of Reading Minds," says that our emotions can lead us to different interpretations of things, people, and circumstances around us. I believe that is true.

With immense pain, confusion, and a troubled mind with the fear of death, the Bible showed itself, or showed aspects, I had never seen before. Those scriptures have gained an have gained an entirely different interpretation.

Our family was going through a very difficult time because our son had undergone a delicate and difficult surgery, just a few days before.

Below I cite some texts that were part of my "conversations" with the Lord. In my anguished expectation for a miracle for our son Rafael, the miracle never happened. Never the way I expected!

These were my conversations with the Father during those days in the Hospital On the morning of April 21, in the process of recovery (already discharged, ready to go home), he suffered a pulmonary embolism and a respiratory arrest.

The state of our Rafael was extremely critical. He was taken away from us. They separated us from him, in the midst of the chaos and sirens going off inside the hospital.

Where was he then? In an Intensive Care Unit, sedated, receiving emergency treatment.

What we most wanted to know in that moment, was when we would be able to know if he had any brain damage and what the extent of it was. When would we know if we would still have Rafa with us or if his brain was gone?

My mind was confused. The pain was (and still is)strange, for I had never felt it before. I've never known such pain. Nothing seems real to me. The people around me are walking very slowly, and their figures are blurred as if I'm in the middle of a dense fog.

Could someone explain to me what happened? He was talking to me just now. Where is my son? My son, my son, my son!

We were going through a day of agonizing and aching wait.

"Hope deferred makes the heart sick, but a longing fulfilled is a tree of life". Proverbs 23:22.

The cry was constant: Lord, what are you doing with our son? Why don't we know anything about him by now? We need to find a thread of hope. If there is hope, we will fight with all our might for it.

And if he is brain dead, what will become of us?

I can feel the absence of his voice. Our house is without music, without his praises. I cannot hear his footsteps coming down the stairs.

I miss him! God, you can heal him, can't you? I know you can! But will you?

The pain has crept inside our chest. The uncertainty of tomorrow is overwhelming.

The procedures to reduce our Rafael's sedation were postponed almost every day; always rescheduled for "tomorrow".

I know, I know, I know, I absolutely know that it is the Lord who decides! I know, too, that He can use the doctors to tell us. I know, I know, I absolutely know that even if the doctors attest to death, the Lord can bring him back. I know! I absolutely know that we will try not to do crazy things. I will try not to revolt at all against the Lord. I will not quarrel with our Savior! But I do not know if I can take it. My wounded, torn flesh wants answers, reasons, an immense desire to assign blame. I must say to my flesh that above and beyond human beings and machines, there is my sovereign God. I need to repeat this to myself! The revolt is growing, like a volcano warning of the impending eruption. My heart is devastated, flooded with pain and sorrow, needing peace. It's bleeding, wanting to attack someone, wanting to explode. I must say to my heart:

"Why, my soul, are you downcast? Why so disturbed within me? Put your hope in God, for I will yet praise him, my Savior and my God." Psalm 42:11.

Mind full of antagonistic thoughts

Images that multiply themselves by the thousands. From his birth, to birthday parties, smiles, his catch phrases (that were his alone), his favorite restaurants, his jokes, his way of being himself. Images that make me grateful for the privilege of being chosen by the Lord to take care of him to this day.

Thirty-one years of the most delightful life of an angel living in our house! However, my mind is also full of revolt. Of a pain that is drugging me, trying to control me and take the ground from under my feet. My mind must find the existential course, the new meaning of life, the new or innovative purpose for me to exist. Above all, when the time comes (I hope and wish it has not yet arrived), to learn how to live with the space (and what large space he occupied), the emptiness on this planet.

My feet hurt, having to step on the cold and hard ground of this mandatory path!

Lord, help!

Our son is still sedated! When he wakes up (we are hopeful he will wake up), we will recognize the Rafa that the Lord has returned to us. Will You return him?

I am very afraid of His sovereignty. Of course, our prayer is for the Lord to give us the same Rafa: cheerful, charismatic, fun, adoring, sweet, who loved God, The Three Stooges, and all the restaurants in the world.

We are still in the valley of the shadow of death. How horrible is this valley. You, Lord, tell us not to fear evil because of His presence with us in the valley. Then why do I feel this immense and intense fear in my soul? Are you not with me in this valley? Are you even with him? Is it only those who are passing through the valley that feel no fear? Because I'm so afraid!

When God works, He is God; when God does not work, He is still God.

How easy it is to sing this song and how hard it is to live by those words.

In these days, in the face of the unknown, of the great fear of losing our son, of the silence that insists on uttering scary cries in the silence of our house, how difficult it is to live. I won't stand it if You don't bring him back!

We are in an agonizing expectation of finding out how the Lord will want us to be in the days to come. Will the Lord give us happy and joyous days? Will we dance and cheerfully worship Him, or will we praise him drenched in tears, which insist on being renewed in a gigantic reservoir. I've never been told that our reservoir of tears is so large.

At dawn, when it is impossible to sleep, Psalm 23 reminds me again. Especially verse 4. ***"Though I walk through the valley of the shadow of death, I will fear no evil for thou art with me; your rod and your staff comfort me".***

Jesus! Please tell me! Why do we have to walk this path? Where are we headed? What awaits us?

"Even if I walked". This possibility has become a fact. We are, in fact, walking down the valley. But this valley is not flat and not even free of stones, stumps, and disgusting bugs. The stones are tearing our feet. The stumps make us stumble and fall. The disgusting bugs attack my mind with poison. They cause vertigo and dizziness. Bugs that cause pain in my head. There are many! I cannot walk anymore. My feet are bleeding. My knees are torn. I'm afraid I'm going crazy. What a horror to have to walk through this valley. Shadows dense, impenetrable, heavy on our shoulders. Shadows that do not allow us to see anything around us, not even in front of us. All we do is try to cling to one another in the tenuous hope that whoever goes ahead, is in turn, clinging to the Shepherd. Darkness penetrates through the pores and strikes the soul and mind. I can no longer see myself, nor recognize myself, in this frightening shadow.

"I will fear no evil"

"I will fear no evil". Really? None? Not a shiver? Then where's my faith? I feel afraid, very afraid. I've got goosebumps on my skin and my legs tremble. I can no longer stop the voices of the spirits, the inhabitants of the shadows, howling in my head with horrible howls. Howls that insist on telling me that death will win.

So, when this corruptible has put on incorruption, and this mortal has put on immortality, then shall be brought to pass the saying that is written: "Death is swallowed up in victory."

"O Death, where is your sting? O Hades, where is your victory?" I Corinthians 15:54,55.

Will someone, some angel or the Holy Ghost, shout this within me, louder than the spirits of the shadow of death? I fear! I fear, Jesus! I confess! Help, I'm afraid.

"Because You are with me". Are you? Where are you Jesus? Is the Shepherd here? Can anyone here feel Him? Because I cannot see, perceive, hear, or feel Him. My eyes are flooded with tears, and I can no longer see. My feet are torn because of the sharp stones of the valley. My knees ripped, because of the many falls on the way. My ears are wide open to the voices of filthy bugs. How do we know that He is indeed? How do we hear His voice? How do we perceive His presence? How do we listen to His word of encouragement? Jesus, why do you stay silent? You seem to like our pain. You seem indifferent to our suffering.

"Thy rod and thy staff comfort me". Your rod, I've felt it! It has come down hard on my back and legs. Your rod has broken my legs. My standing ability no longer exists. How much now, I crawl after Thee, my Savior. I can no longer stand proud before men. All I have left to do is bend over to become the least of all men. Even if I wanted to rise, your rod has already broken my legs and bent my neck.

You know what? Somehow, in a way that I cannot explain to you, I can now feel Your presence. Not because of Your hands, caressing or sustaining me, but because of the rod that blazes in my ears, it cuts off the flesh from my legs and breaks its bones. How it hurts to live on one's knees.

Your staff! Where is it? I need it to be lifted. Without it I will not rise. Your staff! Where is it? Where is it? If Your hands cannot, for the time being, give me breath, at least touch me with Your staff, and please, please, please, bring me some comfort.

You are my Shepherd. Somehow there is still, in the depths of my heart, in distant regions of my soul, in some labyrinth hidden from my mind, a voice that tells me: nothing will fail you! This voice is suffocated by Your silence, which to my ears resembles an indifference. A demonstration that You are not interested in my pain, and not even in the suffering of my son. It does not hurt You at all, does it?

Time and pain

Five days have passed Rafa stopped breathing in my arms and we were still in an agonizing wait. In the painful pursuit of a victory! My son, come home. I miss you so much. Everywhere in the city, by all the streets and corners, buildings and parks, restaurants and churches, lakes and shops, I am reminded of you. In all these empty spaces, you are missing. My longing is hurting so much. The skies of our city cover me with memories of you, my beloved.

Wake up, my beloved! Come back, come home. Come back to me, come back!

The doctors were still struggling to keep him stable and protected from any new infection.

Our prayer that morning was for him to be able to breathe without being intubated. To do so, he would have to overcome the pneumonia that still weakened him greatly. His kidneys were also failing.

If the Lord gave us those victories, we would find out if he was well. If he was still the Rafa we knew.

My heart was turned to Jesus, my Lord. My mind was firm in my Savior. We followed with our eyes fixed on Him, on Him alone.

However, my pain continued to increase. That day, I thought I could not bear it. My back could not (and still can't) be straight, if not curved. My head hung (and still hangs), but my eyes wouldn't even for a second lose sight of Heaven, from where the blessings of my Savior may come.

One more day passed. It was more painful, but I was there, in the presence of the Lord. I know He has collected all my tears (Psalm 56.8). I think He's building a pool in Heaven, it must be! Will He still give us His victory? In any circumstance, the glory will be given to our Savior!

One more day

We were starting another day, another journey, another opportunity, to step on the ground of life's experience.

A rough ground that still caused sharp pain and uttered groans. There was no other rail, no other sidewalk. There was not (and there is not) a way to shorten it and not even how to ask someone to take our place.

Our life was subsisted in spite of the rocky road. Sometimes it seemed slightly stronger, other times extremely faint. Attracting ravenous crows, who insisted on nesting in our heads.

The exercise of walking with broken feet towards a miracle was aggravated by the effort of these scary crows. I could scarcely stop them from flying overhead. But I can prevent them from nesting in my head, I have to; that's why I fight. Even though I can already see a crow delivering bad news in my mind.

Yes! I was afraid! Very afraid. I wasn't losing faith (maybe a little). But I was very afraid of what would come. Fear of living in the empty spaces, places that celebrate the absence of a loved one's life.

Because of fear, I need to be brave. Courage is only necessary when there is fear. If fear does not exist, courage is also non-existent. For courage is the decision to take action, in the environment and in the territory of fear. Act, despite fear. Fear is a feeling. Courage is an action. Courage does not eliminate fear, but it live in you. Fear intimidates courage. But if courage dwells in the recesses of fear, it can act despite where it lives.

For the theologians on duty who will remember: **"There is no fear in love. But perfect love drives out fear, because fear has to do with punishment. The one who fears is not made perfect in love." 1 John 4:18.** The noun "love" here is a reference to God, whose essence is love and throws away all our fear of being in His presence. In the warm atmosphere of true love, one loses the fear of abandonment, betrayal, and injustice. The God who is love throws away our fear of being abandoned by Him.

I will not lose faith. I will not rebel against my Lord. I will not give up hope. I will not miss the blessing of communion with my Lord.

The only thing I want to lose is the pain of losing, which is lost only when losing is lost.

I really want to lose the pain. The pain of seeing my beloved suffer without knowing why. Without understanding the reason, and that makes me sick. It crushes me and revolts me.

I would like to lose the pain that the memory of his suffering face etched in my mind and heart.

How I want this pain to go away. It'll only happen when the pain of my beloved is gone, too.

I cried out, "Arise from thy bed of death, from thy bed of cuts and afflictions, of scares and nightmares. Lift up, my beloved, get up and come to my arms. In my chest you will find your balm, you will find my heart, you will find all my love.

Arise, and embrace me, in an endless embrace full of affection. Let us walk in these new paths, celebrating our love.

Come, beloved son, let us make ourselves drunk in the sweet nectar of love.

Come, my beloved son, let's dance to our choreography of shared passions.

Come, my son, let's watch El Chavo, the Three Stooges, and all the movies.

Let us laugh at ease, not caring about the opinion of the foolish, the boring, and those who do not know what love is, what passion is, what the drunkenness of joy is, or what it is to live intensely. For we know who our Redeemer is.

Wake up my son! Rise up, my love! Come back to me!

The great battles of that day:

• The pneumonia and inflammation of the appendix needed to be overcome;

• Any kind of bleeding, needed to be avoided;

• The surgery needed healing.

Rafael needed a lot of strength. He would face the hard process of decreasing sedation to give us signs that he could be freed from the oxygen machine and then be taken off life support.

It would take more or less 5 hours of agony and feeling of extreme discomfort.

He suffered every minute of it. I was with him to try to communicate with him, and thus to obtain the signals that we so craved. If he understood me, he would answer me properly.

To You Lord Jesus, I raise my prayer. Will today be the day of these victories? Is today the day when the doors of incarceration will be opened and the risk of death undone? Will you bring liberation to our son, my beloved Rafael?

Difficult dawn

On another sleepless night, I opened my Bible and the Word that came to me was:

When He had come down from the mountain, great multitudes followed Him. And behold, a leper came and worshiped Him, saying, "Lord, if You are willing, You can make me clean."

Then Jesus put out His hand and touched him, saying, "I am willing; be cleansed." Immediately his leprosy was cleansed.

And Jesus said to him, "See that you tell no one; but go your way, show yourself to the priest, and offer the gift that Moses commanded, as a testimony to them."

Now when Jesus had entered Capernaum, a centurion came to Him, pleading with Him, saying, "Lord, my servant is lying at home paralyzed, dreadfully tormented." And Jesus said to him, "I will come and heal him."

Lord, Your beloved is dying. This is not a "foreigner," but rather someone who already belongs to You. ONE WORD from You can bring him back from the dark and agonizing jail. It can light his mind up again. Lift him up with life, health, playfulness, and dances with joy! He is Your worshipper.

Our house is silent. The songs he sang to You are muted. Do You not miss them? Do you not desire the voice of this innocent and pure servant?

Bless him with lungs that can breathe.

Do you not wish to see his arms raised in praise? Do you not want to see him dancing to you?

Why do You delay Your healing? Please, just one word, and your beloved will return to my arms.

Lift him up with life, health, playfulness, and dances with joy! He is Your worshipper. This almost fainting father, still with faith and hope, still trusting and persevering, wishes just one word from you. Lord, please tell me, why haven't You sent it yet?

Today they will try to get him off sedation. This will mean hours of agony again. Without sedation he will feel all the pain of the stitches that have ruptured when the resuscitation attempts were made.

Today I ask you to help me pray for a DIVINE analgesic, powerful enough so that our son feels no pain.

Our child will be subjected to an unbearable pain, without the mighty hand of the Lord! O Lord, lay Your hands on that wound!

In the middle of this pain we will know if his brain is healthy! We will know if God's servant will return to his post.

I will need to be with him (and there is no other place in the universe where I would rather be) than with my son!

Today, I trade in all the riches of the world for this one command from You, Lord!

They took out the tubes that help him breathe. He needs to sustain the parameters for an hour. Soon, we can access his brain and see what neurological responses it will give us!

No, no, no! Our Rafa could not sustain his breathing because of the bruised larynx which threatened to close. He had to be re-intubated and given appropriate medication for 72 hours. Then the doctors will evaluate the possibility of doing this again. If this is not possible, a tracheostomy will be the next resource.

We stand before the throne of the Lord at His feet! From His throne the order that will answer our prayers may still come!

May 1st

On May 1st, I went again to the Lord: "Hello Jesus, it was a very difficult day yesterday. I thought that yesterday would be the day that the process of healing for our son would begin. But in my eyes, it was not." The signs were of irreversible damage.

"Can you speak to me through your Word?" Yes, at this moment, with torn backs, skinned knees, and broken feet, I can no longer hear the "prophets." I cannot stand them anymore. I need Your Word. .

Soon afterward, Jesus went to a town called Nain, and his disciples and a large crowd went along with him. Luke 7:11.

You were the Lord of Nain. Would you not like to come to Orlando? More precisely, to Winter Park? Isn't there an "UBER" in the Heavens in which You dwell?

I can imagine this crowd following you.

To follow You is to experience the miracle, the healing, Your unpublished interventions – spectacular, dramatic, sweet, secret, intimate, or in public. Following You means being next to the most powerful source of the maker of blessings and of miracle operations. I think I can see and hear the huge crowd, the shouts of joy and jubilation, added to the cries for help. People crowding the streets, full of hope, convinced of the possibilities of the new, of the intervention that can change the direction and history of our lives. Streets crowded with people, people, people.

Following You means celebrating existence and life. Following You means experiencing the shadow of Your body passing over us, to renew our life, to cure diseases, to eradicate evils and demons, to make the lame walk. By touching Your robe, the bleeding ceases. Receiving the touch of Your fingers makes the blind see and the deaf hear. When we invite You to our homes, children are resurrected. Oh, how I would like to be there right now, with all my family, dancing in the crowd that follows You in the festive caravan of life. But no. That is not where I am today. I am somewhere in the next verse:

As he approached the town gate, a dead person was being carried out—the only son of his mother, and she was a widow. And a large crowd from the town was with her. Luke 7:12.

See this great crowd, Jesus? They are participating in the ceremony that establishes the end of hope, the end of human effort and science, the caravan of death.

The coffin that inaugurates the state of nostalgia, where life begins experimenting with hollow, empty spaces, without meaning, without color, without smell, without sounds, without the object of our deepest love. It is celebrating the beginning of the victory of death, the last breath, the beginning of the decomposition; for he shall become dust.

Here I go. Death has already been stronger. You have given me your punches so many times that I can hardly stand. I'm already staggering in the ring of life. Exhausting all my strength. I have been experimenting the empty places for two weeks, the spaces without his presence or his smile. The abundant and persistent tears in my eyes color this life in gray. There is no sound of his footsteps. There is no sound of his song to the Lord. I have not heard his voice calling me "Palinho, Palinho, Palinho ..."

I already miss his embrace at night and in the morning. Where are his little feet he asked us to massage? How I miss him. And this absence hurts with a pain I have never experienced. And if it gets any stronger today, I will surely succumb.

When the Lord saw her, his heart went out to her and he said, "Don't cry." Luke 7:13.

a. When the Lord saw her! Lord, did you see that mother in tears? Did You see her pain? Did You see her despair? Lord, did you see how her head hung on her chest? The weight of that pain was so heavy. Lord, you saw that right? Do You see me too? And my wife, this mother who already experiences enormous weight on her feet, which make her crawl in the painful path without the presence of her son? Can you see her? If not me, at least her? Look at us, Jesus. Because our eyes are fixed on You.

b. His heart went out to her. Lord, I read that the word "compassion" means "pain in the guts." Did you feel pain in the guts because of that mother and that young man? Do You feel our pain, too? Does it hurt You to see our son dying in pain on that bed? Of course, it does, Lord, I know. There on the cross that You agonized for all of us. But could that cry that you wept, before the fate of Lazarus, sprout again, for us today?

c. You told that woman "Don't cry." I know that wasn't an order but instead a sign that Your miracle would come. Lord, how I would like to hear you say the same thing to me. My eyes are drowning in tears. Soon the tear wells will overflow, forming streams and puddles. I have already shed so many, that in eternity you will not have to dry any tears from my eyes, for there won't be any left. Will You not say the same to my son's mother?

Then he went up and touched the bier they were carrying him on, and the bearers stood still. He said, "Young man, I say to you, get up!" The dead man sat up and began to talk, and Jesus gave him back to his mother. Luke 7:14.

a. Could You, on this day, touch the painful, feverish, bloody bed of my son? Could You stop the wheels of that hospital bed? Please, make it stop. Please stop the furious course of bacteria. Stop the almost indomitable leakage of blood. Stop the course of nature. Just for a moment. Stop! Stop! If you hear me, make it stop!

b. "Young man, I say to you, get up!" Lord, could you do that again? Look Jesus, think carefully: Rafa's case is easier than that young man's. And much, much, much easier than that of Lazarus. Don't You agree? You can. But do You want to? Why won't You answer me? Why do You silence yourself? This silence hurts me, it fills me with bitterness and anger towards You.

c. "The dead man sat up and began to talk." Yes! That's it! Rafa needs to wake up and talk to me. Do you know why? Because after three respiratory arrests during which he was gone for half an hour, doctors say his brain has been damaged. But You know everything there is to know, don't You? Could you make him sit up and talk? Talk, laugh, ask for food, and call me "Palinho" again?

d. "And Jesus gave him back to his mother." Could you deliver Rafa back to his mother today? Lord, can you hear me? Answer me, please. What do you say? Those children in this world are only borrowed for some time? Are you telling me that you raised the widow's son back from the dead and delivered him to his mother just to show me what you will do in eternity with our son? Is this what you're trying to tell me? There the children will be delivered to their mothers forever. Only then will it be forever?

If this is Your answer to me, let me be silent for a little while. As my heavy head hangs over my chest and the ground is watered again with my tears. However, I still know that You can!

Thy will be done on earth (here at home, in that hospital, in our Church, in this city), as in Heaven, where we will one day be reunited with one another forever.

If you, Lord, take Rafa to live with you, would it be okay if when I get there, sometime in the future, that I be welcomed into Heaven by you with your arms around him?

But, just so You know, I still want him here with me! Yet I give him to you, because what's "mine" has always been Yours.

Then fear came upon all, and they glorified God, saying, "A great prophet has risen up among us"; and, "God has visited His people." Luke 7:16.

a. "Then fear came upon all...." May His will make this city fearful of God. Especially among the Brazilians who live here.

b. "And they glorified God..." May Rafa's life be an instrument of God to help people glorify Him.

c. "A great prophet has risen among us;" I know this was a reference to Jesus Himself. But if our life and our death can have any meaning on this planet, make of us, of our home, of our home, a home whose lives prophesies Salvation.

d. "God has visited His people." Visit us, Lord! If it's Your will, visit him in that hospital bed. Then come to our home and our city. May Your people feel visited by You through all that is happening to us.

Rafael was in great danger. He had pneumonia, inflammation of the appendix, was breathing with the help of machines, and was without any real sign of a healthy brain. Part of his stitches from surgery ripped off, opening the entire suture, expelling blood. The fever could not be overcome until today. Up until yesterday, his body did not respond to the antibiotics. There is still a great concern that another blood clot might make its way from his arms to his lungs.

Great is the miracle we seek. Great is the fear of the Lord which we hope for.

Rafael, you are in the hands of God, from where you have never left.

Yes! We still believe, we still hope, we still fight, we still look only up.

Yes! Our faith also teaches us (with immeasurable pain) to pronounce: MAY THE WILL OF GOD BE DONE!

Death's caravan was shocked by life. The caravan of life overcame that of death. It replaced death with life and both caravans became one of JOY, DANCE, PRAISE, AND LIFE.

Please send a caravan of angels, playing trumpets, harps, and lyres (drums too, because Rafa is very fond of playing the drums) to meet this caravan, which has not yet invaded the streets of the city, but which already announces its path with some lights turned off.

In my caravan of pain and fear, I stretch my neck, I fix my eyes, I listen carefully, in the burning expectation of seeing

You in the distance. But all that I perceived from the Lord was a gruesome impression of death. What difference does it make to a dying body, as it was mine, to take another punch, another fall? Are you listening to me, Lord?

May 2nd

On May 2, 2017, the doctors warned us: "Rafa is suffering from septic shock." Another blood clot has entered his lungs, removing his chances of living off the oxygen tubes. His brain is deeply damaged. Bacteria are attacking him uncontrollably, hence the septic shock. There are no more chances. He is no longer here. There is nothing else to do.

The doctors told me that I could choose between keeping him in a coma, tubed and waiting for the bacteria to finish its job, or letting him go. My answer, which came out in screams of pain was: "Doctor, please let him go! Please let him go"! They asked me to make the worst decision of my life. Only I could authorize the shutdown of the machines and let him go to the Lord. It was the most painful experience of my life. Rafa was disconnected from the machines and his clogged lungs stopped almost immediately. However, his strong heart still beat for an hour and a half, until it stopped.

My daughter Camila and I, stayed with him until his last minutes with the sounds of hymns of praise. Camila held one of his hands and I the other. We were crying, caressing, and kissing his face and wetting his chest with our many tears. We waited for the moment of his last breath, which would send him through the portals of eternity, and send us into a life to be experienced in streets where houses, trees, birds, people, and buildings are painted dark gray.

We were minutes away from tasting the bitter taste of his absence, and our emotions were shredded, in the dark, gloomy, and hideously silent reality of a space to be experienced without our beloved.

An hour and a half later, he gave his last breath and slept, slept, slept. Before my eyes, with my embrace, kisses, and tears. Tears that are still abundant right now as I write these lines.

Today, May 2, 2017, at 9:30 p.m., our son Rafael, at age 31 and 7 months, changed his address! He went to live with the Lord Jesus. He lent us an angel, and now he's taken him back home! See you, son! One day we will meet again and then, it will be forever!

5. THE CRUSHING in Gethsemane

GOD AND HIS SON; MY SON AND I: MEANING AND PURPOSE.

There I was on the dawn following the departure of our Rafael, trying to hear a word from God. How presumptuous of me. Lord, Lord, Lord of my life. Lord of my house. Lord of my belongings. Lord of this Universe, built and sustained by You. My Lord and my God! When Your son Jesus was on the Mount of Olives, He went and prayed leaning on a stone called "Gethsemane." I know that Gethsemane is not a place, but a stone. It is not the name of a village, town, or city. It's the name of a stone.

It is a stone – today, there is a temple in that location – which is situated at the foot of the Mount of Olives in Jerusalem, Israel, where it is believed that Jesus and his disciples prayed the night before His crucifixion.

According to the Gospel of Luke, the anguish of Jesus in Gethsemane was so deep that His sweat became great drops of blood, which ran down to the ground.

"And being in anguish, he prayed more earnestly, and his sweat was like drops of blood falling to the ground." Luke 22:44.

These were carved stones, so that they could hold many sacks with the fruit of the olive tree. The first sack held the weight of 5, 6, or 7 sacks that were put on top so that the bottom one was slowly crushed, making the first pure olive oil. The extraction was slow and painful. The slowness of the crushing was the only way to extract the purest, most expensive, and most palatable olive oil.

There, His Son, Jesus, leaned over, and no longer bearing the weight of the sins of all mankind, began to be crushed. The suffering of Jesus did not begin when he was imprisoned. It began in heaven, when he left his throne because of you and me.

On that day, on the Mount of Olives, when You leaned on that stone, with the weight of my sins, added to the sins of all mankind, it slowly crushed You in a torturous and unspeakable pain. You, my Lord, being tortured and crushed, slowly and painfully, began to release Your purest, most expensive essence. From your sweat came great drops of blood that ran to the ground. There, the Lord shed His sweat and His blood because of the slow and painful crushing that lay on his back. Those first wounds were the medicine that would cure me of all diseases, whose source is sin.

"But He was wounded for our transgressions, He was bruised for our iniquities; The chastisement for our peace was upon Him, And by His stripes we are healed." Isaiah 53:5.

You did something with Abraham when You asked for his beloved son Isaac. You let Abraham climb the mountain with his son who was asking where the animal was for the sacrifice. Abraham knew who would be sacrificed. But he did not dare tell his son. Then, at the moment of the sacrifice, when the knife was to be lowered with extreme violence, You held Abraham's hand. He offered You the lamb, a symbol of Your son who would later come as the Lamb of God who takes away the sin of the world. To Abraham, you have returned his son! You did that again with the son of the Shunammite woman: returning him to his mother. And then again with Talitha: returning her to her parents. And again with the young dead man, the son of the widow of the city of Nain; You brought him back to his mother. And finally, Lazarus: You returned him to his sisters.

You did not do the same to me or to my son's mother and sisters. I know you will do it in eternity, when we all meet. I know. But here, on this earth, in this world, the Lord chose not to do the same with us. Why not us? I don't know. I don't even know if I need to know, I only know that You are God! You are God!

In fact, Lord, just as you did not do it with the little boy found dead on that beach. After he tried to flee his country at war. You did not do the same with the Coptic Christians of Egypt, beheaded by ISIS. You did not do the same with the Syrian children killed by chemical weapons. No! You did not do the same. I wonder why? But I don't need to know Your motives and plans. You are God!

As for me and my son? What did you intend, my Lord and God, to do to us by crushing us, in a dreadful and agonizing slowness of those fifteen days in the hospital?

You crushed Rafael. A human being so pure, a believer in You, an intercessor, a genuine worshipper. Someone who loved life so much.

He loved singing, smiling, and playing with people. He remembered all the birthdays and anniversaries, he sent his messages full of love and simplicity. He never fought or hurt anyone.

What did You want, Lord, by crushing him so slowly? Lord, Lord, not only the purest oil you could extract from him, but also his own life, his soul, his being. Everything in him, and he, himself, was distilled by the indomitable crush that fell to his body.

You were and always are in control of everything, right? You are God! You are God!

So I can blame You for everything you've done to my son, right? You are responsible for all that. You are! You are!!!

Was that it? It was Rafael's soul that you wanted, Lord? Was that it? So (here goes the creation trying to argue with his Creator) why didn't You just make him go to sleep?

Did you have to crush him like that? Tell me, did you? The screams of pain, fear, fright, and the confusion that overtook him, before having a respiratory arrest in my arms. Seeing him shouting at me: "Dad, Dad, I'm afraid, it hurts, my head, help me, help me, help me..." When he could no longer speak, he beat me hard in my chest, as hard as he could, crying desperately for help which I could not give him. I could not give him such help. I could not free him, while his eyes of despair and fear hurt my own eyes and heart.

This impotence consumes me in accusations and guilt and defeat. It was the pulmonary embolism that attacked him relentlessly.

Of course, you've always been in control. But what about me? You were there, serene, quiet, with everything under Your absolute control. You looked like a cosmic torturer. How am I going to deal with all this within myself?

Then Rafa stopped in front of me in my hands. There would still be another cardiac arrest, and another, and another. The worst moments of horror and fear, despair and screams, that my wife and I never thought we'd experience with our loved one.

Tell me Lord, how did you feel? In the struggle for survival, our son was afflicted with pneumonia, appendicitis, and bacteria. Finally, he had another pulmonary embolism.

Lord, I know you were in control. You are God! You are God! But what about me? How am I going to deal with this? Does the God who claims to love me and love my son, torture him with constant wounds, one after the other, in a growing and indomitable wound?

If You love me, is it really true that if we ask in His name, the Lord will do it? If we knock on the door, it will open? Because to me, Lord, You shut it, slammed it in my face, and locked it. You turned off the lights of your house to make me think that there was no one there. What did you want with my house? Lord, did You not realize that by crushing Rafael in the stone of Gethsemane of that hospital, you would be crushing everyone in our house? Of course, You knew. But would there be no other way to crush us? No?

What did you want to extract from me? Nothing good I suppose, for there is nothing good in me. Unless you wanted to extract what I do have: malice, deceit, lies, anger, hatred, selfishness, greed, laziness, etc.

Or maybe you wanted to extract from my soul the desire for success, fame, applause, and recognition. Now, I ask you: What for? Why would you extract all this stored dirt, well hidden in the dark and icy holds of my mind? Why enlighten all these uninhabitable, disgusting, fetid labyrinths that make up my being? All these deep and dark places of my being, which I had already covered, painted, and decorated with the adornments and disguises of my religiosity.

Everything was whited out. Why did the Lord want to get

there? And worse, why did you want to bring it all out?

Was it to embarrass me, in front of the audience that watched the crushing? Was it to destroy my reputation and redeem my character? Was it to destroy my religiosity and build spirituality? Would it be to erode my selfish motivations (often thinking of what I would gain in return) by serving others, making me, forcing myself to serve with genuine love, who surrenders for love of God and love of people? Or would it be to teach me that all my compassion in these 35 years as a Pastor was not a legitimate, truly human, truly spiritual, and holy compassion? Could all my compassion for the tragedy of mankind be just a role I interpreted by virtue of my priestly garments? Was that it?

Yet, stubbornly, I ask you, Lord, would there be no other way? Could you not just have crushed me? Without touching your angel, who in our house dwelt for these so few 31 years?

Crushing him, as the Lord did in that "Gethsemane," to the point of making him go and dwell with you, still crushed me!

Now, the empty places, crush me. His room without sounds and without music, crush me. The absence of his voice, crushes me. No longer hearing his laughter and his singing, crushes me. To see a simple object that belonged to him, crushes me. Not receiving those calls from him, asking: "Daddy, are you almost home? How long is it going to take?" The phone is mute from his voice and it continues to crush me, killing me.

Until when, Lord? Until when my Lord, my God? You are God! You are God!

I gave you my son, in deciding to turn off the machines that pretended to give him life. Because of that, because of that decision, I blame myself every second.

I gave You my son, on the mountain of painful adoration, to see him slowly stop breathing and his heart stop, as I hugged him screaming in horror and fear.

Seeing him slowly stop, again, in my hands. Before, not by my will, now, by my consent.

How do you, Lord, think I'll handle it? How, for Your sake, tell me. You are God! You are God!

Now, what I have left is myself, who surrenders to You now, as I did yesterday, and will do tomorrow.

What will remain of me, without shells, without appearances, without priestly garments, without disguises, without social / political / religious attitudes? Just a remnant of me. If this is what you wish to have, then take what is left of me, for You! After all, no one else will want someone who is no longer an acceptable partner / politician / religious figure. In a way, I am "glad" for this "freedom" of being only what I am, what remains. The Lord gave him to us, and with such joy we had him. The Lord took him, in an extremely painful way. To the Lord is in the most intense way, our gratitude for the privilege of having been Rafael's parents. May He be glorified today and forever! Amen!

"Father, why hast thou forsaken me?"

You know, Jesus, I suppose you were forsaken because of Your life's purpose. Your purpose in this world was to be our Savior, right?

But what about me and my son? Will you save somebody through all this? From that auditorium with more than 1,200 people, in celebration of Rafa's life, will you save someone? Of the 15,000 people who watched his celebration online, will you save someone? Will you do something for someone?

You are God! You are God! My Lord, my God!!! You, God and Your son Jesus ... my son and I... sense and purpose!

6. EXPERIENCING THE PAIN *of a loss*

I still cannot say what mourning is to me. Three months after the departure of our son, we are still only touching it, with the tips of our fingers. I wish I could (boldly) pinpoint where I stand within the classic so-called cycle of mourning.

However, my experience (which obviously can be unique and absolutely private) in facing the loss of a child, has been marked by great confusion and a mixture of feelings.

In a general sense, with a few differences or nuances, the authors who write about the subject make reference to phases they consider to be part of the process of mourning.

In this process, I am not going from one phase to the next, as the so-called "stages of mourning" presuppose. On the contrary, these "phases" blend together inside me. Dull my ideas, intoxicate my eyes, tingle my fingertips, weaken my legs. My readiness to read (I usually read two or three books a month) disappears.

Feelings of guilt, bitterness, and anger towards God feed my flesh, and at certain moments, I have feelings that bring me closer to my son, in a strange, sickly and dysfunctional relationship of love.

Despair pushes me to abandon the pastoral function. Especially when it comes to moments of praise in the church. On such occasions I will "see" him there, singing and dancing as he always did. Then, a horrendous dread and intense desire to give up those moments instills itself, without resistance, in my heart and soul. My guts squirm when I try to make myself look calm in front of people.

Immense pain puts me in absolute discomfort before people who seek me for counseling. In a way, they sometimes seem not to remember my own pain. Or they believe that because I am a Pastor, I am already "well" (my quest to study and try to understand the human soul, to listen with love, empathy and compassion about the pain of others, has always been one of my greatest passions in life).

When they begin to talk, I catch myself comparing their pain with mine. I become inwardly impatient, inwardly attacked.

People saying things like, "I'm worried because my wife spends too much money, or “I can’t find a job,” or “I'm praying for a new house,” or “I need to buy a new car,” or “My children are disobeying me,” or “I want to find a boyfriend,” etc. I have to put in a lot of effort (this effort exhausts my physical and mental strength, completely draining my energies) into listening with love, passion, respect, and empathy, to the people who stand before me. After all, every pain is intense because the human body reacts to the least exposure of pain. Therefore, although their pain may be smaller than mine, the reaction that the human organism promotes is absolute. Hence, the pain of each one is total and absolute because the reaction is absolute as well.

Unfortunately I have learned that I am not, have not been, and will never be the only one to experience such pain.

I have learned that today, I can (absolutely against my will) tell people who go through such an experience: "I think I can understand you!"

From day one, I have wanted to isolate myself from everything and everyone. In fact, I sometimes wish the world would stop living, laughing, celebrating. Does no one understand that my son has died? How can people still laugh, go to restaurants, parks, theaters, and football games? Stop it! Stop it!

Today, three months after my son's death, I want people to live normally.

I wish for the world to open the doors of bars, restaurants, theaters, football stadiums, and city parks.

Why do we need (or just want) to isolate ourselves?

From the earliest days on, we have been experiencing an

appalling sense of being a type of cause for the "discomfort of others."

When I arrive, or we go as a couple to any place, people change. They are embarrassed. They are uncomfortable. They do not know what to say, they do not know what to do. It's as if I could read their thoughts: "Should I get up? Should I address him? What do I say? Should I hug him? Can I continue eating? Can I continue my joyful conversation with my friends? Should I pretend I did not see them? Should I put a somber mask of on my face?"

It seems that other parents, when they look at me, feel fear and horror at the possibility of losing a child as well. They want to avoid me, for I have become a walking advertisement of the possibility of tragedy. It seems that people are afraid of being infected with my "disgrace." I know all this may just be a wrong impression. But that's how I feel sometimes.

In these environments, we are tempted to flee, disappear, isolate ourselves from everything and everyone.

Accepting the facts? It hurts to wake up from the nightmare and realizing it was not a nightmare at all, but the harsh reality. Rafa is gone. He no longer exists in this world. He will not call me again and say, "Daddy, are you coming home already?" I try to listen to the skies, I try to hear Rafa's voice telling me: "Daddy, I'm fine. Everything is fine with me. I'm waiting for you to get home. Here at home. In our eternal home."

Acceptance is there only because there is no other possibility. You either accept, or you accept. A revolting, non-conforming acceptance.

Peace, relief, restoration, reconstruction? Yes! But just because there is no other way. There is no other way to move forward.

I do not like living without Rafa. My longing for him destroys me. It destroys my desire to exist and to thrive. In the better moments, we have doses of consolation which warrant us hours of relief, some strength, a little hope for ourselves. The hope we will learn to live this new phase of our lives. The hope we will find the existential course, the (new) meaning of life.

I do not want to be strong, nor brave. I'm not superhuman. I am not some sort of "Marvel" character of religious fantasy, who teaches that the Shepherd is a man endowed with supernatural abilities. Fantasy that makes me insensitive to pain, indifferent to love, an owner of a sexual organ muffled by some "magic potion" found on the shelves of divine communion. Denying the creation of the Creator and consequently denying the Creator of creation.

I am not, and I will never wish to be, a figure of evangelical religious folklore whose pathetic smile, like a wax statue in a museum, is the super pastor, or superhuman.

I want to be human, flesh and blood. No! No! I'm neither strong nor brave. I am weak. Why, for God's sake, do people

want me to be strong and brave? The scripture says that **"when I am weak, then I am strong" (2 Corinthians 12:10).** So why, right now, when the Lord has given me the grace and privilege of being weak in myself and strong in Him, do people want to take away the privilege of the raw and real humanity of being weak, weakened?

I want to cry all the cries, moan all the moans, scream all the screams until I lose all the strength in me.

For me, those classic "stages of mourning" go something like this: I have discovered that mourning does not divide itself into logical phases. It has not been like this for me.

You do not overcome the shock, the trauma of watching your child stop breathing in your arms, asking you to help him, and you could not do a thing. One does not move from a phase of revolt, simply, to despair, then withdrawal, and then to understanding, and lastly to acceptance. At least not in my case.

What you feel is an overwhelming and stunning mixture of all those feelings. All at the same time, without any logic, order or mercy.

Pain, revolt, confusion, anxiety, refusal, anguish, depression, suffering, guilt, anger, desire to place blame, isolation,

resignation, apathy, loneliness, despair, thoughts of death, wishing for death. A non-acceptance of the fact, revolt with the irreversibility of the fact, and revolt against God, turn into a pill that must be swallowed every day.

At this point, it's been three months that I cannot hear his voice, his songs, his laughter. I no longer have his company. All this pain, trauma, and all these absences, stab my heart and mind, making it impossible for the so-called last phase of mourning to come near me. Understanding, peace, relief and restoration? No, not yet. Would my infinite love for my son allow me to be happy again? As if nothing had happened?

7. MY OPINION (TODAY) ABOUT BOOKS THAT NARRATE *Similar cases*

Evidently, I have not read every book about losing a child. But the ones I have read (the ones that tell a story) testify to the fact that each case is different and unique. Those who have gone through the loss of a loved one, especially parents who have lost a child, seldom have a similar process of mourning.

And the testimony, or account of each case, may perhaps be of any help in cases that are very similar.

It is not helpful, at these times, to hear or read the stories of other cases. Almost always, hearing other stories of loss only increase pain and revolt. It is almost impossible not to compare their pain with our own. We end up finding many differences between their situation and ours.

The best consolation, the best help, is to be close to those who have suffered the loss, and to listen. Do not talk. Just listen.

Testimonies and written stories are a better source of help for the authors themselves, as they expose and "document" their love for the person they lost. I have found it is not very helpful when other parents, in the midst of their pain, are encouraged to read about other people's loss.

I believe that an account, a testimony, or a book about losing a child will mainly serve for parents to know that all those feelings are normal.

When we give advice on how to overcome and adjust, in most cases, we only increase the pain of those people. In addition to everything they are feeling, they are carrying more frustration: they cannot overcome their own pain. And in worse cases, those couples feel guilty. They feel guilty for their inability to overcome. There are even those who feel extremely offended when we try to help them overcome their pain. They interpret the absence of pain as a statement, a testimony that the love they felt was too small, for the pain was soon over. I've already caught myself thinking that my pain should be forever – always gigantic, it must be the size of my love for my son. Of course, this is not so. However, many feel this way.

When we try to let them know of other cases, or help them "overcome" their pain, they feel as if we are violating what they carry most sacred. When writing this book – about

Rafa and my pain – my intention is not to console, but to show how my pain has been. The anatomy of my pain. The purpose of the book is to say: each one suffers in his own way, in his own time. The story of your life is sacred and only yours!

Books should help us understand that there are multiple ways to experience grief, to experience pain, and confusion of feelings.

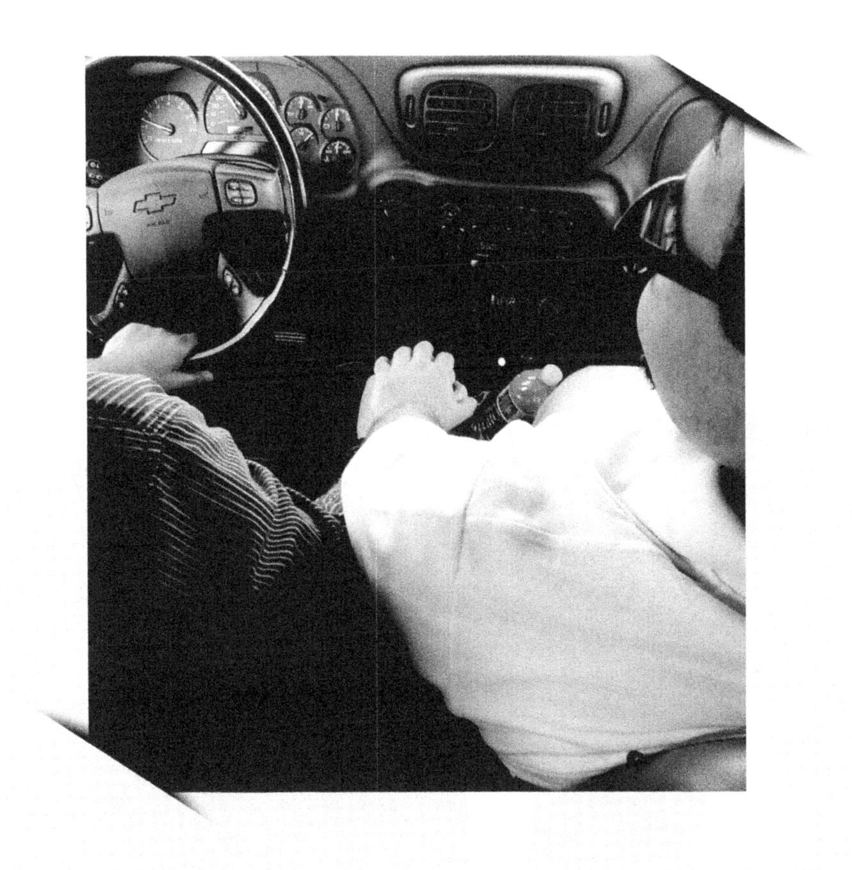

The greatest role of books written by other parents who have lost a child should be to help us avoid creating a one-size-fits-all process of therapy! I see myself enriched by everything I read. However, my main blessing in reading and listening to other accounts has been to discover that there are no universal models, neither of suffering nor of therapeutic processes, that will be suitable for everyone.

The titles of most books should be changed from "How to overcome" and "How to be healed" to titles like: "My pain," "My Story of Love and Loss," and such. Many books help us realize that our pain and personal reaction is not wrong!

The way some people excel, win, and rebuild their lives will never be the norm for others.

In my opinion, the purpose of all the books that tell the story of losing other people should be: suffer your mourning with freedom, do not keep your feelings to yourself, give yourself time, as much time as you wish, you will find your new path, you will learn to live with your pain.

FINAL *Considerations*

WHAT NOW?

Rafael has always been my companion. He always went to the office with me. On days when he didn't come, he kept calling: "Daddy, are you coming home now?" One, two, three, and even four times he would call me asking if I was coming. Now when I come home, I keep the phone in my hands, waiting for his call, but it never comes, and it will never come again. Driving my car and resting my right hand on the console, without his left hand resting on mine, hurts too much. Going to church and looking at the places where he used to sit, and which are now vacant, hurts. The silence at home, without him singing praises; his side of the couch, now empty, hurts too much. It hurts too much! I miss him so much! Today our hearts bear immeasurable peace (mixed with fear and unconformity) and a void of the same size. There are moments of dense darkness all around us, marked by a horrible silence. Moments when memories of the days in the hospital crush us so cruelly that we think it will be impossible to bear. Amidst the darkness and silence, amidst the thunderstorms that dwell in our minds, our Lord takes our hands, giving us a little strength to take the next step, helping us to look forward, filling our hearts with peace and some joy. Our request to God, every second, has been for Him to teach us to live the days to come, one day at a time.

We are once again experiencing the days, weeks, and months of dense darkness we experienced in the first months of Rafa's life. Again, we are moving around blindly, stunned, hurt, wounded, sick, discontented, and angry. We are living our second mourning.

Thirty-one years ago, we had to bury the idealized child and live the pain and confusion of mourning. In these days, when we have buried the accomplished son, again we experience the mental pains and confusions of mourning. For 31 years and 7 months, we have learned how to take care of a baby. We settled for the fact that we had a baby. We usually raise children, send them to college, watch them get married and have children of their own. Rafa was different. Perhaps without noticing, Lucia and I orbited around him. Our reason for living was his dependence upon us. Suddenly he was taken away from us. What now? How do we live without him? How do we find meaning in this darkness?

We began the journey of new learning. Lucia will live only for me.

I will live only for her.

But how could we not cry in bed because of his absence? As we lie down, how can we not keep our eyes on the door of our room, aching with longing, knowing that he will not come as he did every night, to kiss us, to hug us good night?

Thirty-one years ago, we were on dark paths. We were gradually being guided. Gradually, the darkness gave way to light. Gradually, our path, once tortuous and painful, became a flicker of light, of joy and celebration, of caresses and love that left us intoxicated.

Our hope is that, again, the Lord will dispel the darkness and shine a light that will illuminate our minds and hearts, helping our eyes find a new reason to live, a new meaning to life.

Now, when we face the overwhelming pain of longing, will the Lord also help us? Will it be that in these darkness-covered streets, in this dense darkness, the Lord will lead us again?

We believe so! We believe so! We need him to.

For the pain, the longing, the non-conformity, the anger, the feeling of having failed to help, all of this haunts me and fills my desire for the Lord to abbreviate my days on earth, so that the doors of eternity will be opened wide, offering me an early reunion with the beloved of my soul.

When pain crushes everything inside, once again the world around loses purpose, loses color, loses its flavor, we lose the desire to continue existing. Depression installs itself in the soul, mind and heart. A deceitful depression, which fools us by appearing to be warm and friendly. It is not really an antidote to pain, but venom that expands pain.

Lord, I need, I want to restore my sight, my hearing, in order to see a world still with colors, smells, tastes and sounds of joy.

How I wish I could dance again! My feet are still broken. My legs are still torn. My back is still hunched over, my head is still hanging over my chest. How do you dance like that? What other dance, but that of nostalgia?

Will you help me, Lord? I'm sure You will!

THE HEAVENS

What do we know about the Heavens? Very little! The Bible says that Rafael sleeps with the Lord. The Bible says that the dead will rise and those who are alive on that day of the appearing of the Lord will be together again for all eternity.

I do not know what Heaven is like. I think the Lord allows us to "form" a perfect expression of Heaven, based on what we like here on earth.

So taking the liberty of becoming an "inventor" of my Heaven, I can see him playing drums in a band, going to all the chain restaurants of Heaven.

I will see him, not a "baby," but a strong man, beautiful and perfect. There in the sky I can have my 1998 BMW Z-3 in "perfect condition." Rafa will ride it with me (at full speed, because we can no longer die). We'll be laughing! He'll have his hand upon mine, as he did here in this world. I know he'll say to me, "We can eat as much as we want here, dad!"

I know he's going to invite me to watch an Orlando City game because he's their number one fan. Rafa will tell me: "Palinho, let's go to an Orlando City match, shall we? Here, they play very well!" (This is our tribute to our glorious Orlando City).

So when we are together, in our eternal home, we will be embraced: Bruna and Camila, my daughters; Gilson, my son-in-law; Gabriel and Thomas, my grandchildren; Lucia, my wife; and me. All of us hugging Rafa. This time it will be forever! Until that day, I will continue here, crying with longing, knowing that it does not pass with time. Could you, Lord, do with us, as you did with King David?

"Make me hear joy and gladness, That the bones You have broken may rejoice." Psalm 51:8.

Why does all of this still hurt so much? For we were not created for death, but for life. Death is an assault and at the same time, it is a "backfire." Death, which attacks us, tries to rob us of life, is betrayed, and is deceived. For it, death, serves only in the end, as an instrument that leads us to the true life: ETERNAL LIFE. What a wonderful privilege. What an indescribable privilege the Lord has given us, when we have borne an angel. What a wonderful privilege. What an indescribable privilege it was to live in the flowery paths, full of music, laughter, and the uniqueness of our son. That angel lived in this house. Now you have changed his address. He went to a place so beautiful and so big that it has room for us too.

My soul has always longed for the Savior calling me by name. From now on, my soul also yearns, with moans and pains, for the day when I will hear from you again, Rafito: "Palinho, Palinho, Palinho." Then you will take my hand again and bring it to your face. If this wait is only a few more minutes, it will feel like thousands of years to me. Today I tell you: See you soon, son! See you later, Rafito. Palinho will be home very soon. I'm coming! And our embrace will be eternal.

Afterword

1. See you soon, my son!

(September 20, 2017, Rafa's birthday)

Vinícius de Moraes, the author of many writings, poems, songs, and enchanted words, has also written a farewell sonnet. I read it today, and seeing his words on paper, where he recorded his pain and despair, I thought: "Today is the birthday of my son Rafael, who on this date would be 32 years old but death is only for those who in the Creator and Savior do not believe. For to us who believe, my son is alive – more alive than ever, and in his eternal abode, where he is surely celebrating with a great party. I thought about writing my own "sonnet:"

Farewell Sonnet

Hi son, Palinho here...

Suddenly from laughter there was weeping,

When your silence became my cry, my pain and my dread ...

The deafening sound of your silence, muted all the other sounds of the city, the singers and the worshippers.

And from your hand, which no longer rests on mine, I can only be astonished.

See you, son!

Suddenly the calm, with which you were taken, turned into furious wind in my downcast mind, in my broken heart, in my emotions, wrecked my joy ... forever. Will it always be like this?

See you, son!

When your eyes closed, mine were filled with a dense fog that still confuses my steps.

My formerly happy eyes, when they saw yours, now blind without the brightness of them, stumble in the unevenness of the path that is mandatory for me.

See you, son!

That morning, after your cries for help, asking me to save you, were suffocated by the call of Grace that was making you cross the portals of eternity, I was left with the pain of parental incompetence. But it will not be like this forever. It will not be like this forever.

I could not do what only God could do, and He did not want to.

And from your immobility came my drama, my fate, my destiny, void of any happiness.

See you, son!

I became the lover without love.

But it will not be like this forever. It will not be like this forever.

See you, son!

You were always so close and demanding of me, now you live far, in a city from where you cannot come back ... And it will be forever. It will be like this forever.

The adventure that it was to live with you, is now only a constant look at the boring hours. To see if they pass faster, so I may see you again.

And I know that suddenly, no more than suddenly, I will see you again. This time it will be forever. It will be forever!

You can no longer call me asking, "Are you coming, daddy?" But my heart can hear your voice crying out for my arrival.

I promise you, son, I'm on my way, I'm almost at the door of your new home.

I'm on my way, son! I'll be there soon, son! And it will be forever!

"Palinho".

2. LONGING

Six months of missing you! This week, in an old castle in the mountains of Sintra, as I looked into the distance through one of the arches of the castle, this longing crushed me so hard! So, I cried on paper and I'll share it with you.

"After you left, my world has become "almost":

Almost colorful,

Almost beautiful,

Almost pleasant,

Almost interesting,

Almost cheerful,

Almost good to live in,

Almost, almost, almost, but never completely.

Except, almost completely uninteresting,

Almost completely meaningless,

Almost completely discolored,

Almost completely boring,

Almost completely bad to live in,

Almost completely sad,

Almost completely without you, because of your memories I am completely enveloped, I am completely consumed, I am completely writhing myself, I am completely fed up, I completely desire you back in my arms.

But as I absolutely know you will not return to me; I absolutely know:

That you are well,

I absolutely know that you are happy,

I know, I absolutely know that you are healthy,

I know, I absolutely know that you wait for me,

I know, I absolutely know that I will go to you and with you ETERNALLY I will be,

With you eternally I will live,

With you eternally, I will be embraced,

With you, eternity will be full of affection, kisses, laughter and hugs;

Then all of the "almosts" will be gone and our reunion will be an eternal gift!

3. Bruna, my daughter, wrote this about Rafael:

I still find it very strange to talk about my brother in the past. Partly because I'm scared to leave him there, and partly because part of me still wants to believe that maybe, just maybe, it was all a mistake and that he will walk through that door at any second, only this time for real and not in another dream.

When we were little, he used to take my dolls and throw them off the couch. He loved to watch them fall from the seat to the floor, and he'd do it for hours. Sometimes they would break, and I would run to his room, furious, ready to argue with him. He always frustrated me because he never fought with me; he'd wait until I was done with my speech and then just say "I'm sorry." And that was it. And it would always be like that with anyone else who was crazy enough to argue with him. Because not even the tiniest fiber in in his body was evil and he didn't know what "grudge" even meant.

My brother was better than everyone else. He was funnier, cooler, more loving, and more original than anyone you know, and I feel sorry for those who did not have the good fortune to know life with him.

His absence is felt every day, in this emptiness and silence that he left with us.

I love you, Rafa, and I cannot wait to hug you again.

Your Bruna.

4. Camila, my other daughter, also wrote something about Rafa:

"... long life I will give you ..."

In these last six months, I have "lived" in the book of Psalms, read and reread expressions of pain, joy, frustrations, hope, but above all, expressions of praise.

And how else could I keep your image in my memory if not through praises? The honesty of the psalmists reminds me of you, who always with such simplicity, expressed what you felt and poured it at the Savior's feet.

I have been given complete freedom to feel the same feelings that the psalmists felt, without any reservation or shame, but doing what you did best, living in full, experiencing the pains and joys of this life, with eyes focused up high.

I confess that I still do not understand everything that God has done and is doing. Sometimes other psalms come to my mind, especially on days when my thoughts are too messed up to organize themselves. "Turn my eyes away from worthless things; preserve my life according to your word" (Psalm 119.37), "Blessed are those whose strength is in you, whose hearts are set on pilgrimage. As they pass through the Valley of Baka (tears), they make it a place of springs; "(Psalm 84: 5-6).

Although I do not understand, there is a deep conviction within me that, as with everything that was related to you, this will also be great and magnificent. And I would have loved for you to be here to celebrate all that God is going to do.

But God has chosen to reveal to you the glory of him completely, and to us only a few glimpses, for now.

What is left for me is to live and witness what is to come. To love those who have loved you so much and to bear your memory with them forever. Long life, my brother, even if only

in our memories. Long life, till at last we may enjoy eternal life together.

Camila or, "Fifia," as you liked to call me.

5. TEARS IN HEAVEN

"Tears in Heaven" is among Eric Clapton's most personal songs. He co-wrote with Will Jennings about the intense pain Clapton experienced following the death of his four-year-old son, Connor, who fell from a window on the fifty-third floor of an apartment building in New York City.

Would you know my name

If I saw you in heaven?

Would it be the same

If I saw you in heaven?

I must be strong and carry on

'Cause I know I don't belong here in heaven

Would you hold my hand

If I saw you in heaven?

Would you help me stand

If I saw you in heaven?

I'll find my way through night and day

'Cause I know I just can't stay here in heaven

Time can bring you down, time can bend your knees

Time can break your heart, have you begging please, begging please

Beyond the door there's peace I'm sure

And I know there'll be no more tears in heaven

Eric believed that Heaven was not his eternal home. The unimaginable pain of the loss of a child, aggravated by the "certainty" (or fear) of knowing that he did not belong in Heaven. Which destined him to live eternally separated from his son. Eternal pain.

My pain is temporary, because my Savior, because of His Grace (only that and nothing else, nothing in me, because there is nothing good or acceptable in me), guarantees me the eternal reunion with my son. And so, I will never again be torn apart.

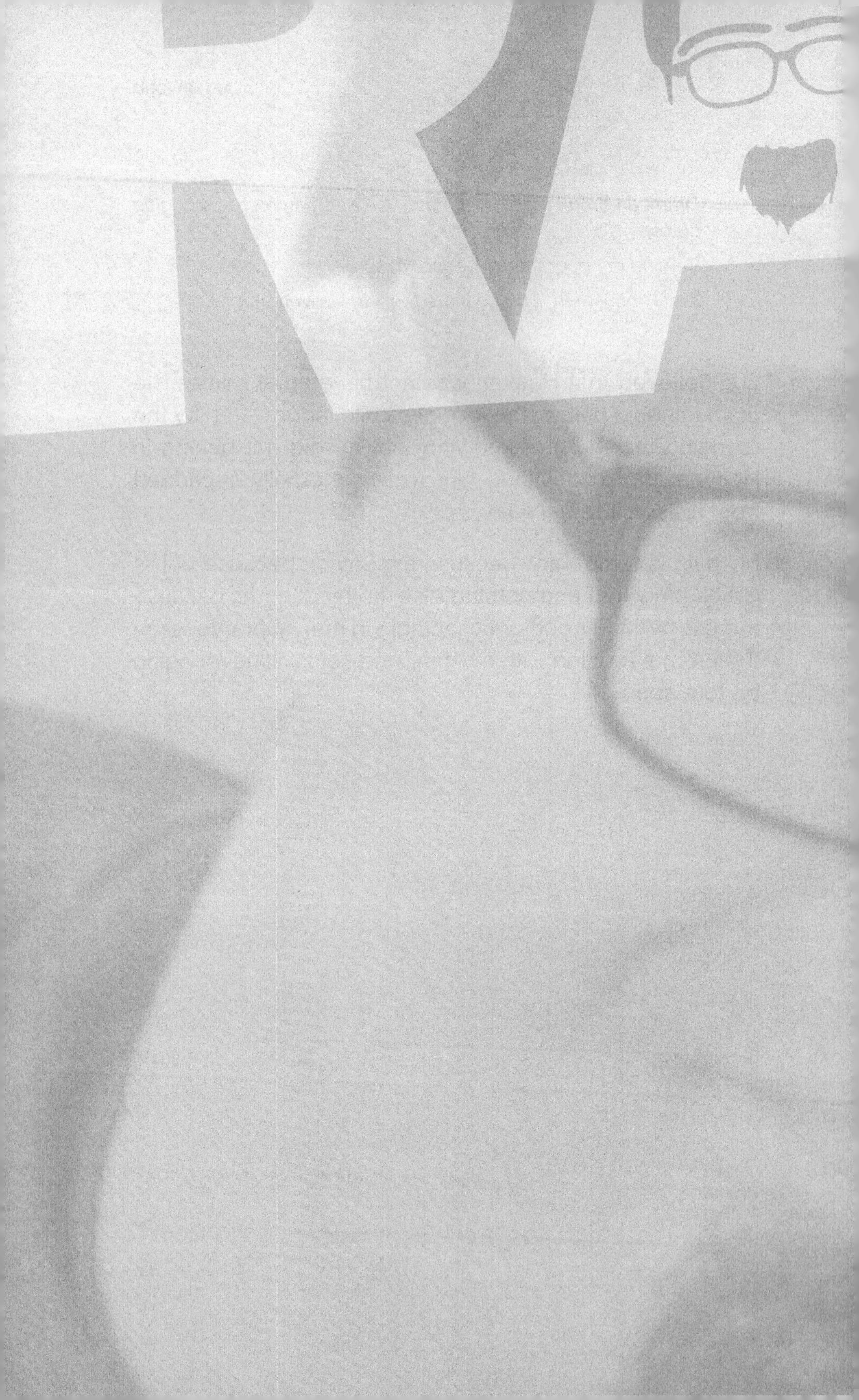

ABOUT THE AUTHOR

Nivaldo Nassiff was born in São Paulo, Brazil, on December 9, 1955. He's been married to Carmen Lucia Nassiff since October 11, 1980, with whom he had three children: Camila Garcia Nassiff - December 21, 1981, Rafael Garcia Nassiff - September 20, 1985 - moved to Heaven on May 2, 2017, and Bruna Garcia Nassiff - April 17, 1989. He has a PhD in Clinical Christian Counseling, a master's Degree in Clinical Christian Counseling, and a Bachelor's Degree in Clinical Christian Counseling from Florida Christian University; he obtained his Bachelor of Theology from Theological Baptist University of Perdizes / São Paulo. He is a Pastor linked to the Order of Baptist Pastors of Brazil of the Brazilian Baptist Convention. He planted the First Baptist Church of Parque São Rafael, in São Paulo. He was Pastor of the Vila Prudente

Baptist Church, São Paulo. He started the ministry CENA - Evangelical Community Nova Aurora, which helps addicts, prostitutes, convicts, and others. He started a church in the city of Florida, Uruguay, from 1989 to 1991. He was one of the pastors of the First Baptist Church of Curitiba and senior pastor of the First Baptist Church of Greater Boston. In 2010, he became the senior pastor at Global Village Church. He now serves as the pastor of Brazilian Ministries of the First Baptist Church of Orlando.

From 2000 to 2002, he represented Latin America for missionary work at SIM - International Society of Missions, and INTERSERVE, an agency specializing in bringing professionals to poor communities around the world. In Brazil, this institution is called "Latin American International Partnerships - ALPI".

He is the author of "Learning to Evangelize with Jesus Christ". Associate Professor of "Acts 1:8 in Action," - Transcultural Missions courses in local churches in Brazil and Latin America. Professor / Supervisor of Hospital Clinic Chaplaincy by ACCC - The Association of Certified Christian Chaplains. He is a lecturer of diverse themes related to human development.

Made in the USA
Columbia, SC
16 November 2022